Woman's Day®
BEEF, VEAL
AND LAMB

Sedgewood® Press
New York

The following material was adapted from a previously published book and is used by permission of the publisher: Best-Ever Gravy, Sirloin-Tip Roast, Stuffed Breast of Veal, Veal-Shoulder Roast, Roast Leg of Lamb reprinted with permission of Macmillan Publishing Company from *Jack Ubaldi's Meat Book* by Jack Ubaldi and Elizabeth Grossman. Copyright © 1987 Jack Ubaldi and Elizabeth Grossman.

Photographer Credits

Ben Calvo: pages, 24, 38, 47, 50,57, 86, 110
George Contorakes: pages 81, 82, 83
John Paul Endress: page 58
Katrina Filary: page 16
Michael Molkenthin: page 19
Michael Skott: page 120
Tim Turner: pages 13, 23, 44, 78, 98, 116
John Uher: pages 4, 9, 14, 20, 26, 31, 34, 37, 39, 40, 42, 48, 49, 51, 52, 53, 54, 60, 64, 65, 67, 68, 70, 73, 75, 84, 88, 90, 94, 96, 102, 106, 108, 115, 117, 118, 122

Please address your correspondence to Customer Service Department, Sedgewood® Press, Meredith Corporation, 150 East 52nd Street, New York, NY 10022.

For Hachette Magazines, Inc.

Food Editor: *Woman's Day:* Elizabeth Alston
Researchers: Mary Rieger, Marinella Cancio

For Sedgewood® Press

Director: Elizabeth P. Rice
Editorial Project Manager: Maryanne Bannon
Editorial Director: Alison Brown Cerier
Project Editor: Miriam Rubin
Copyeditor: Joan Michel
Designer: Remo Cosentino
Production Manager: Bill Rose

ISBN 0-696-02351-2

Library of Congress Catalog Card Number: 90-061941
Printed in the United States of America
10 9 8 7 6 5 4 3 2 1

Contents

RECIPE SYMBOLS

At the beginning of many recipes are symbols
pointing out which dishes are:

♥ **LOW-CALORIE** (main-dish serving under
300 calories)

🕘 **MAKE-AHEAD** (part or all of the recipe can
or should be made ahead)

✳ **MICROWAVE** (recipe or variation)

★ **SPECIAL—AND WORTH IT** (in terms of
time, calories or expense)

Beef Roasts and Pot Roasts

Cooked to a turn or simmered in a succulent gravy, a beef roast makes any occasion special. With a few ingredients and a minimum of preparation, dinner cooks by itself—leaving you free to enjoy other things.

Sirloin-Tip Roast with Skillet-Roasted Onions; Scalloped Potatoes with Green Onions

Roasts

☐ **Is It Done?** Cooks have traditionally tested roasts for doneness by poking, patting or piercing the meat. While all these methods work with some success, the best way to tell if a roast is done the way you like it is by checking the internal temperature with a meat thermometer when the estimated cooking time is up.

There are two types of meat thermometers. The first has a fat stem and is inserted into meat before the roast is put in the oven. The second, the narrow-stemmed instant-read thermometer, is placed into meat toward the end of the estimated cooking time. It is not designed to bake in the oven, so don't leave it in while roasting. To check the temperature, remove roast from the oven or pull out the oven rack and insert the thermometer. If it's not done yet, remove thermometer before continuing to roast.

Although the first type of thermometer is convenient, it may conduct heat to the interior of meat too rapidly. When the thermometer is removed, it leaves a large hole, so juices leak out. The instant-read thermometer makes a much smaller hole, so less juice is lost. However, try to insert it in the same place if testing meat more than once.

Whichever thermometer you decide to use, for an accurate reading always insert it in the thickest part of the meat, not touching bone or in a fat pad.

☐ **Beef Roasting Chart:** These estimated cooking times are based on meats roasting in a 300° to 325°F oven, with the exception of tenderloin, which is usually roasted at 425°F.

Because of the heat retained in the meat, the internal temperature will continue to rise after the roast is removed from the oven. Take out small cuts when the internal temperature is 5 degrees below desired serving temperature, larger roasts when the internal temperature is 10 degrees below desired serving temperature.

Carving a Beef Rib Roast

☐ Remove loosened chine bone (backbone). If necessary, remove a wedge-shaped slice from the large end of roast so meat will sit firmly on carving board. Insert a fork below the top rib and carve across the "face" of the roast toward the rib bone. Cut along rib bone with tip of knife to release slice of meat. Slide knife back under slice of meat, steady it with the fork and lift slice to a serving dish.

Cut	Weight (lbs.)	Temperature	Minutes per lb.
Rib Roast	4 to 6	140°F (rare)	26–32
		160°F (medium)	34–38
		170°F (well)	40–42
Rib Roast	6 to 8	140°F (rare)	23–25
		160°F (medium)	27–30
		170°F (well)	32–35
Rib Eye Roast	4 to 6	140°F (rare)	18–20
		160°F (medium)	20–22
		170°F (well)	22–24
Tenderloin	2 to 3	140°F (rare)	45–50*
Tenderloin	4 to 6	140°F (rare)	45–60*
Rump Roast	4 to 6	140° to 170°F	25–30
Tip Roast	3½ to 4	140° to 170°F	35–40
Tip Roast	6 to 8	140° to 170°F	30–35
Top Round	4 to 6	140° to 170°F	25–35

*total cooking time, not minutes per pound
Source: National Live Stock and Meat Board

☐ **Roasting Less Tender Cuts:** The most tender roasts come from the rib or the loin, but they're the most expensive, too. The less tender (and less expensive) cuts, such as rump or tip roasts, often have more flavor and can be successfully roasted. First, choose meat with good marbling, small veins of fat running through the meat, which help keep it moist and tender. You can also use a marinade with an acidic ingredient, such as vinegar, wine or lemon juice, to tenderize the meat. Cook the meat only to the rare or medium-rare stage for best flavor and tenderness, and slice very thinly across the grain.

☐ **Standing Time:** In many of our recipes the meat stands for about 10 minutes after removal from the oven or grill. Standing time is very important: As the meat rests, the juices redistribute throughout and the temperature rises 5 to 10 degrees depending on the size of the roast. After standing, the roast will be evenly cooked, juicy and done to a turn. It will also be easier to carve, because it "relaxes" as it stands. Large cuts usually do not need to be covered during standing time because they won't cool off quickly. But if the kitchen is cool or the cut is small or thin, cover the meat loosely with a foil tent or a sheet of foil while it stands. Never cover the meat tightly because it will steam. Some juices will seep out of the meat during standing. Pour them over the sliced meat or add them to the gravy; they are full of flavor.

Fillet of Beef Madeira

Madeira, a fortified wine, adds body and richness to this sauce. Use the dry Madeira served as an aperitif, not the sweeter denser version sipped with dessert. Serve this special dish with boiled new potatoes and buttered carrots sprinkled with chopped fresh mint.

4 tablespoons butter or margarine
One 2½-pound boneless beef tenderloin
**   roast, trimmed of all visible fat**
½ teaspoon salt
¼ teaspoon pepper
4 large mushrooms, sliced
3 tablespoons finely chopped shallots
**   or white part of green onions**
½ cup dry or medium-dry Madeira wine
1 can (10¾ ounces) beef gravy

1. Turn on oven to 425°F. While oven heats, melt 2 tablespoons of the butter in a shallow roasting pan in oven.

2. Turn roast in butter to coat evenly. Season with salt and pepper. Roast 45 to 50 minutes, until a meat thermometer inserted in the thickest part registers 135°F for rare. (Roast longer if you want meat more well done.) Remove roast to a cutting board and cover loosely with a sheet of foil to keep warm. Let stand 10 to 15 minutes; internal temperature should rise to 140°F. Pour off fat from the roasting pan; set pan aside.

3. Meanwhile, melt remaining 2 tablespoons butter in a large skillet over medium-high heat. Add mushrooms and cook 4 minutes, tossing frequently, until they give up their liquid.

4. Add shallots and cook 3 minutes, stirring frequently, until tender. Add Madeira; bring to a boil and boil 1 minute.

5. Stir in beef gravy and bring to a boil. Reduce heat to low and simmer 15 minutes.

6. Pour Madeira sauce into defatted roasting pan. Place pan over medium heat and bring to a boil, stirring to scrape up browned bits on bottom of pan. Pour into a sauceboat.

7. Slice roast and arrange on a heated platter. Serve with sauce on the side.

Makes 8 servings. Per serving: 543 calories, 21 grams protein, 4 grams carbohydrate, 48 grams fat, 115 milligrams cholesterol with butter, 98 milligrams cholesterol with margarine, 438 milligrams sodium

Standing Rib Roast with Sautéed Mushrooms

A grand dish for celebrating holidays, a promotion at work or Sunday with the family. Serve with pan-roasted or mashed potatoes and steamed asparagus. Apple pie with ice cream would be an all-American finale. Remove a piece of meat this large from the refrigerator a half hour before roasting to take the chill off.

One 12- to 13-pound standing rib roast
**   (about 5 ribs), trimmed of excess**
**   fat (see Note)**
1½ teaspoons salt
½ teaspoon pepper, or to taste
8 large mushrooms
For garnish: fresh parsley sprigs or
**   other fresh herbs (optional)**

1. Heat oven to 325°F. Have a large shallow roasting pan ready.

2. Rub roast with salt and pepper. Place fat-side up in roasting pan (no rack is necessary; ribs form a natural rack).

3. Roast about 2½ hours, until a meat thermometer inserted in the thickest part, not touching bone, registers 130°F for rare (ends will be medium to well-done) or 150°F for medium.

4. Remove roast to a heated platter or a cutting board. Let stand 15 minutes; internal temperature should rise 10 degrees.

5. Meanwhile, place roasting pan with drippings over medium-high heat. Add whole mushrooms and cook 3 to 5 minutes, turning once, until crisp-tender and browned. Remove from heat.

6. Carve roast and arrange on platter. Lift mushrooms from pan with tongs, letting fat drip off. Place mushrooms around roast and garnish with herbs, if desired, and serve.

Makes 8 servings with leftovers. Per 4-ounce serving with 1 mushroom: 287 calories, 33 grams protein, 1 gram carbohydrate, 16 grams fat, 106 milligrams cholesterol, 243 milligrams sodium

Note: For best-quality meat, look for a rib roast cut from the large end, not the small end. Have the butcher loosen the chine bone (backbone). After roasting, remove it for easier carving.

Roundup Roast

Serve this impressive roast with a pile of corn on the cob grilled in the husks. First soak the corn in cold water 30 minutes. Drain and grill on the barbecue 15 to 20 minutes, turning occasionally, until husks are charred and kernels tender. Wear gloves to pull off the hot husks.

1 cup strong black coffee
1 cup orange juice
1 large onion, chopped (about 1 cup)
1 tablespoon dried rosemary leaves
1 tablespoon dried thyme leaves
1 teaspoon pepper, plus additional pepper
One 5-pound lean boneless beef top round or
      tip roast, trimmed of excess fat
½ teaspoon salt

1. Mix coffee, orange juice, onion, rosemary, thyme and the 1 teaspoon pepper in a large bowl or a double plastic food bag. Add beef; cover bowl or close bag. Marinate in refrigerator, turning roast several times, at least 6 hours or up to 2 days.

2. Prepare barbecue grill or heat oven to 450°F. To prepare grill: Set an 11⅝x9¼-inch foil drip pan in bottom of barbecue. Arrange about 25 briquettes around the outside of each long side of drip pan. Light coals. When coals are hot and completely covered with gray ash (about 45 minutes), pour ½ inch water into drip pan.

3. Drain roast; reserve marinade.

4. To grill: Place roast directly on grill rack over drip pan, 4 to 6 inches above hot coals. Close grill hood or cover roast with a loose foil tent. Grill 1½ to 2 hours, turning and basting roast with reserved marinade six times, until a meat thermometer inserted in the thickest part registers 130°F for rare. (Grill longer if you want meat more well done.)

To roast: Place meat on rack in a shallow roasting pan and roast 1½ to 2 hours, turning and basting roast with reserved marinade six times, until done as described.

5. Remove roast to a cutting board. Season with salt and additional pepper. Let stand 15 to 20 minutes; internal temperature should rise to 140°F.

6. Cut meat in thin slices, arrange on a heated platter and serve.

Makes 12 servings. Per serving: 219 calories, 37 grams protein, 2 grams carbohydrate, 7 grams fat, 102 milligrams cholesterol, 175 milligrams sodium

Herbed Rump Roast

You can make a sensational salad by tossing thin strips of leftover roast with slices of red onion, avocado wedges, capers and a red-wine vinegar and olive-oil dressing.

1 large clove garlic
1 teaspoon salt
1 teaspoon paprika
¾ teaspoon dried basil leaves
One 3-pound boneless beef round rump
      roast, trimmed of excess fat

1. Heat oven to 325°F.

2. Mash garlic with salt, paprika and basil to an almost smooth paste with the flat side of a heavy chef's knife on a cutting board or with a mortar and pestle. Rub into beef.

3. Brown beef in a Dutch oven over high heat, starting fat-side down and turning until browned on all sides.

4. Cover roast partially with a sheet of foil. Transfer to oven and roast about 1½ hours, until a meat thermometer inserted in the thickest part registers 130°F for rare. (Roast longer if you want meat more well done.)

5. Remove from oven. Remove foil and let stand 10 minutes; internal temperature should rise to 140°F. Transfer roast to a cutting board. Skim fat from pan juices. Cut roast in thin slices and arrange on a heated platter. Spoon pan juices over meat and serve.

Makes 8 servings. Per serving: 431 calories, 29 grams protein, 0 grams carbohydrate, 31 grams fat, 117 milligrams cholesterol, 338 milligrams sodium

---

Using Foil in the Microwave

Foil protects food from overcooking because it reflects microwave energy.

☐ Use foil to shield areas of food that would cook too quickly, such as the edges of a roast and wing tips on a chicken, and to cover the corners of square dishes.

☐ Keep foil smooth, close to food and at least 1 inch away from oven walls and door to prevent arcing—a spark between two metal points. If arcing does happen, just open the oven door and flatten the foil or move it away from oven walls. Arcing is not dangerous, but it can damage oven walls.

Microwave Rosemary Roast Beef with Pan Gravy

✳ MICROWAVE

Microwave Rosemary Roast Beef with Pan Gravy

If you've never tried cooking a roast in the microwave, you'll be amazed by the results.

**One 3-pound boneless beef bottom
    round roast, tied, trimmed of
    excess fat**
1½ teaspoons minced fresh garlic
**1½ teaspoons chopped fresh rosemary
    leaves or 1 teaspoon dried
    rosemary, crumbled**
¼ teaspoon pepper
¼ teaspoon salt
Pan Gravy (recipe follows)

1. Rub roast all over with garlic, rosemary and pepper. Place on a microwave-safe roasting rack with sides or in a shallow 11x7-inch microwave-safe baking dish. To prevent overcooking: Shield the roast by smoothly molding 1¼-inch-wide strips of foil around the outside cut edges of the roast. Insert a microwave-safe meat thermometer, if you have one, in thickest part of meat.

2. Microwave uncovered on medium-low 30 minutes, rotating dish ¼ turn twice. Remove foil, turn roast over.

3. Microwave 25 to 30 minutes longer, until the temperature registers 130°F for rare.

4. Remove roast to a cutting board and season with salt. Cover with a loose foil tent to keep warm. Let stand 15 minutes; internal temperature should rise to 140°F. Skim fat from pan juices; reserve juices for gravy.

5. Cut roast in thin slices and arrange on a heated platter. Serve with Pan Gravy on the side.

Makes 4 servings with leftovers. Per 4-ounce serving: 214 calories, 35 grams protein, 0 grams carbohydrate, 7 grams fat, 102 milligrams cholesterol, 87 milligrams sodium

Pan Gravy
1⅓ cups beef broth
2 tablespoons all-purpose flour
Defatted pan juices from roast
⅛ teaspoon pepper

1. Whisk ¼ cup of the broth with the flour in a 4-cup microwave-safe measure until smooth. Gradually whisk in remaining broth, the pan juices and pepper.

2. Microwave uncovered on high 4 to 6 minutes, whisking once, until thickened. Pour into a sauceboat and serve with roast.

Makes 1½ cups. Per ¼ cup: 137 calories, 2 grams protein, 2 grams carbohydrate, 14 grams fat, 19 milligrams cholesterol, 206 milligrams sodium

Sirloin-Tip Roast

(Shown on page 4)

The beef round tip weighs about 14 pounds. Trimmed and left whole, it is a beautiful football-shaped roast, but it is usually cut in 6-pound pieces and sold as sirloin-tip or silver-tip roasts. Serve this roast with Best-Ever Gravy and Skillet-Roasted Onions.

Sautéed vegetables from Best-Ever
    Gravy (see Best-Ever Gravy,
    below)
One 6-pound boneless beef sirloin-tip
    roast, tied, trimmed of excess fat
  ¼ teaspoon salt
  ¼ teaspoon pepper
Water
Best-Ever Gravy (recipe follows)

1. Heat oven to 350°F. Have ready a large roasting pan with the sautéed vegetables.

2. Season roast with salt and pepper. Place on the vegetables in roasting pan. Pour 1 cup water into pan.

3. Roast 1½ to 2 hours: 15 minutes per pound for rare—a meat thermometer inserted in the thickest part will register 130°F; 20 minutes per pound for medium, 150°F. Turn the roast two or three times during cooking, adding more water if necessary to prevent vegetables from burning.

4. Remove roast to a heated platter. Cover loosely with a foil tent and let stand 10 to 15 minutes; internal temperature should rise 10 degrees. Meanwhile, make the gravy.

5. Transfer roast to a cutting board and remove strings. Carve across the grain in thin slices. Serve with Best-Ever Gravy on the side.

Makes 8 servings meat with leftovers, 1½ cups gravy. Per 4-ounce serving with 3 tablespoons gravy (with oil): 460 calories, 26 grams protein, 1 gram carbohydrate, 37 grams fat, 112 milligrams cholesterol, 123 milligrams sodium

Best-Ever Gravy

  2 tablespoons butter, vegetable oil or a
    combination
  1 medium-size onion, coarsely chopped
    (about ¾ cup)
  1 medium-size carrot, coarsely
    chopped (about ¾ cup)
  1 medium-size stalk celery, cut in ½-
    inch pieces (about ½ cup)

1. To sauté vegetable mixture: Melt butter in the roasting pan over medium heat. Add vegetables and cook 3 to 5 minutes, stirring two or three times, until onion is nearly tender. Remove from heat and proceed as recipes direct.

2. To make gravy: Spoon vegetables and pan juices into a food mill or a strainer set over a saucepan. Press through food mill (do not use a food processor; the resulting purée will be much too thick). In strainer, press with the back of a wooden spoon to extract juices. Discard vegetables. Skim off fat.

3. Place saucepan over medium heat and simmer juices until hot. Pour into a sauceboat and serve with roast.

Note: For thicker gravy: For each cup of strained juices, mix 2 tablespoons all-purpose flour or 1 tablespoon cornstarch with ¼ cup water until smooth. Before simmering, gradually stir mixture into juices, then stir until gravy boils and thickens.

Skillet-Roasted Onions

(Shown on page 4)

To peel a large quantity of fresh small onions, first loosen skins by immersing them in boiling water for 5 to 10 seconds. Drain in a colander and rinse under cold running water. Trim the ends and slip off the skins and the first layer of the onion.

  ¼ cup butter or margarine
  1 pound small fresh white onions,
    peeled, or frozen onions,
    unthawed
  ⅛ teaspoon salt
  ⅛ teaspoon pepper

1. Melt butter in a large skillet over medium heat. Add onions and cook 10 minutes, shaking pan or stirring often until onions are browned.

2. Cover and cook 8 minutes for frozen, 15 minutes for fresh, stirring occasionally and reducing heat if necessary, until onions are tender. Season with salt and pepper.

3. Serve hot.

Makes 4 servings. Per serving: 144 calories, 2 grams protein, 10 grams carbohydrate, 12 grams fat, 35 milligrams cholesterol with butter, 0 milligrams cholesterol with margarine, 221 milligrams sodium

Great Meal-Makers

Any of these three side dishes—rice, potatoes or barley—adds delicious essential complex carbohydrates to your dinner without making preparations more complicated. Oven cooking guarantees even cooking—there's no stirring, no watching—and all three go beautifully with any roast you choose to make.

To add a vegetable bake-along, just open a package of frozen vegetables into a baking dish, add 3 tablespoons of water, season with salt, pepper and an herb you like, cover and put in to bake about 25 minutes before you plan to serve the roast. The vegetables will be ready at the right moment.

Scalloped Potatoes with Green Onions
(Shown on page 4)

To cut calories, we made these without butter or flour. To avoid boil-overs, fill the baking dish no more than two thirds of the way.

- 1½ **pounds all-purpose potatoes, peeled and cut in ¼-inch-thick rounds**
- 2 **cups sliced green onions**
- 1¾ **cups milk**
- ½ **teaspoon salt**
- ¼ **teaspoon pepper**

1. Heat oven to 350°F.

2. Layer half the potatoes and half the onions in a 13x9-inch baking dish. Repeat layers. Pour in milk and season with salt and pepper.

3. Bake 1 hour, until potatoes are tender when pierced with a fork. Remove from oven.

4. Serve hot.

Makes 8 servings. Per serving: 102 calories, 4 grams protein, 18 grams carbohydrate, 2 grams fat, 7 milligrams cholesterol, 163 milligrams sodium

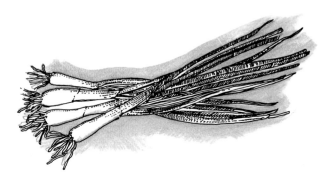

Lemon Rice

- 2 **tablespoons butter or margarine**
- 1½ **cups uncooked long-grain white rice**
- 1 **teaspoon whole mustard seed**
- 3 **cups chicken broth**
- 3 **tablespoons finely chopped fresh parsley**
- 3 **tablespoons grated Parmesan cheese**
- 1 **teaspoon grated fresh lemon peel**
- 2½ **tablespoons lemon juice**

1. Heat oven to 350°F.

2. Melt butter in a large ovenproof skillet over medium-high heat. Add rice and mustard seed. Cook 3 minutes, stirring frequently, until mustard seed starts to crackle and rice is translucent. Add broth and bring to a boil. Remove from heat.

3. Cover skillet; transfer to oven and bake 20 minutes, until rice is tender. Remove from oven.

4. Add parsley, Parmesan, lemon peel and juice to rice. Stir with a fork to mix and fluff rice.

5. Serve hot.

Makes 5 cups, 8 servings. Per serving: 169 calories, 4 grams protein, 29 grams carbohydrate, 3 grams fat, 16 milligrams cholesterol with butter, 7 milligrams cholesterol with margarine, 322 milligrams sodium

Barley Pilaf

- 3 **tablespoons butter or margarine**
- 1½ **cups medium pearl barley**
- 1 **large onion, finely chopped (about 1 cup)**
- 3 **cups chicken or beef broth**
- 1 **tablespoon finely chopped fresh parsley**

1. Heat oven to 350°F.

2. Melt butter in a 3- to 3½-quart rangetop-to-oven casserole over medium heat. Stir in barley and onion and cook 5 minutes, stirring frequently, until barley starts to brown. Add broth; increase heat to medium-high and bring to a boil.

3. Cover casserole. Transfer to oven and bake 1 hour, until barley is tender.

4. Remove from oven; stir in parsley and serve.

Makes 5 cups, 8 servings. Per serving: 185 calories, 5 grams protein, 32 grams carbohydrate, 5 grams fat, 19 milligrams cholesterol with butter, 5 milligrams cholesterol with margarine, 327 milligrams sodium

Pot Roasts

☐ **The Kindest Cut:** There is nothing more satisfying on a cold winter's day than a fragrant, stick-to-the-ribs pot roast. To end up with a delicious, juicy pot roast, you need to start with a suitable cut of meat. The cuts we recommend will make a flavorful roast because they come from the well-exercised muscles of the chuck section, providing sufficient intramuscular fat for moisture. Supermarkets use various names for the same cuts, cautions the National Live Stock and Meat Board. To help decipher them, here are the three cuts that are recommended for pot roasts plus some of the other names you may find on the package label.

Boneless Beef Chuck Cross-Rib Pot Roast— also known as Boneless English Cut, Boneless Boston, English Roll

Boneless Beef Chuck Shoulder Pot Roast— also known as Boneless English Roast, Boneless Shoulder Roast, Honey Cut

Boneless Beef Chuck Eye Pot Roast— also known as Boneless Chuck Roll, Boneless Chuck Fillet, Inside Chuck Roll

All of these cuts are usually sold tied, so they will hold their shape while cooking. Slice off all but a very thin layer of exterior fat before cooking; this can be done without untying the meat. If the meat isn't tied, trim off excess fat and tie with white string at 1-inch intervals to make a neat roast.

☐ **Meaty Options:** Wide flat pieces of meat, cut like very thick steaks, may also be cooked as pot roasts. The cuts in this category include Seven-Bone Chuck Pot Roast, Top Blade Roast and Chuck Blade Roast. While the flavor is good, these cuts will not give you the same large, even slices as the three recommended pot-roast cuts above. For cooking, you may have to use an oval-shaped pot or a heavy roasting pan rather than the traditional round Dutch oven. Snip the connective tissue in several places so the meat doesn't curl up while cooking; trim away bone and gristle when carving. Because the cuts are thinner, cooking time may be significantly shorter. When the meat is fork-tender, it's done.

☐ **Safekeeping for Pot-Roast Leftovers:** Never leave cooked meat at room temperature longer than two hours. Leave leftover meat in one piece so you can cut, slice or cube it—whatever a recipe requires. Wrap meat tightly in plastic or foil or place in an airtight container. When using plastic food bags, press out as much air as possible before closing. Store gravy separately; pour it into a shallow container so it cools quickly. Use cooked meat within three days, gravy within two days. Reheat leftovers thoroughly, covering meat to retain moisture. Bring gravy to a rolling boil before serving.

☐ **Cooked Just Right:** Cooking time can vary as much as 30 minutes depending on the shape and thickness of the roast. To check for doneness: Pierce the meat with a fork; it should feel tender and offer no resistance. If in doubt, cook it longer.

Pot Roast in Mock Mole Sauce

Authentic Mexican mole sauces are complex taste symphonies containing several different dried chiles, sesame seed and/or almonds and twenty or more other seasonings. Made with ingredients readily found at the supermarket, this easy streamlined version hits the high notes—it's nice and spicy but not very hot. Leave some seeds in the peppers if you want to set off the fire alarm. Leftovers, if there are any, make a terrific taco filling.

- 1 tablespoon vegetable oil
- One 4-pound boneless rolled beef chuck shoulder pot roast, trimmed of excess fat
- 2¾ cups chopped onions
- 1 tablespoon chili powder
- 2 teaspoons dried oregano leaves, crumbled
- ¼ teaspoon ground cloves
- 1½ teaspoons coarsely chopped fresh garlic
- 2 tablespoons tomato paste
- 12 ounces regular or full-flavored nonalcoholic beer (not light beer)
- ⅓ cup thinly sliced green onions
- ¼ cup chopped seeded fresh jalapeño peppers or other mild or hot pepper
- 1½ teaspoons unsweetened cocoa powder
- ½ teaspoon salt

1. Heat oil in a Dutch oven over medium-high heat until hot but not smoking. Add roast and brown well on all sides. Remove to a plate.

2. Add onions to Dutch oven, stirring to scrape up browned bits on bottom. Reduce heat to medium-low. Cook onions about 20 minutes, stirring often, until very soft and browned.

3. Stir in chili powder, oregano and cloves, then garlic and tomato paste.

4. Return roast to Dutch oven. Pour in beer and stir to mix with onions and spices. Increase heat to medium-high and bring to a boil. Reduce heat to low. Cover and simmer about 2½ hours, until meat is very tender when pierced with a fork. Remove from heat.

5. While roast is cooking, mix green onions and jalapeño peppers in a small bowl.

6. Transfer meat to a cutting board. Cover loosely with a foil tent to keep warm.

7. To make sauce: Skim fat from juices in Dutch oven. Process in a food processor or a blender with cocoa powder and salt until smooth.

8. Cut beef in thin slices and arrange on a heated platter. Spoon sauce over meat. Scatter onion-and-pepper mixture over the top and serve.

Makes 6 servings with leftovers. Per 4-ounce serving meat with 2 tablespoons sauce: 445 calories, 28 grams protein, 5 grams carbohydrate, 33 grams fat, 104 milligrams cholesterol, 111 milligrams sodium

Pot Roast in Mock Mole Sauce

Sharpening Knives with a Steel

Hold the steel firmly in the left hand (if right-handed). Hold the knife in the right hand, placing the heel of the blade at a 20-degree angle to the steel. Draw the blade downward across the steel until the entire length of the blade has passed lightly over the steel. Repeat the same action, this time with the blade on the other side of the steel. Alternate this procedure five or six times on each side.

Braised Pot Roast with Wine and Fruit

Use a red wine good enough to serve at the table, such as a burgundy, Chianti or Merlot. Most of the alcohol in the wine evaporates during cooking, but if you prefer you may replace the wine with 1 cup unsweetened purple grape juice, ½ cup water and 2 tablespoons red-wine vinegar. The dried fruits add a mellow flavor. Mashed potatoes and Brussels sprouts are good side dishes for this roast.

One 4-pound lean boneless beef chuck
    cross-rib pot roast, tied, trimmed
    of excess fat
½ teaspoon pepper
2 envelopes (¾ ounce each) brown-
    gravy mix
1½ cups dry red wine
¼ cup orange juice
2 medium-size red onions (about 5
    ounces each), each cut in 8
    wedges
½ cup loosely packed dried apricots
½ cup loosely packed pitted prunes
Two 2-inch-long bay leaves

1. Heat oven to 325°F.

2. Rub meat all over with pepper.

3. Put gravy mix in a Dutch oven (not uncoated aluminum). Stir in wine and orange juice until smooth. Place over medium heat and stir until sauce is boiling and very thick. Remove from heat.

4. Add meat to Dutch oven. Scatter onions and fruits around meat. Add bay leaves.

5. Cover pot and transfer to oven. Bake 3 to 3½ hours, until meat is tender when pierced with a fork.

6. Remove pot from oven. Uncover and let stand 15 minutes.

7. Transfer roast to a cutting board and remove strings. Cut meat across the grain and arrange on a heated platter. Discard bay leaves from sauce. Spoon some of the sauce and fruit over the meat; pour the remainder into a sauceboat and serve with roast.

Makes 6 servings with leftover meat. Per 4-ounce serving meat with ⅙ of the sauce: 651 calories, 33 grams protein, 26 grams carbohydrate, 18 grams fat, 118 milligrams cholesterol, 462 milligrams sodium

Microwave Method: Reduce amount of pepper to ¼ teaspoon. Reduce amount of wine to 1 cup. Increase orange juice to ¾ cup. Deeply pierce roast all over with a two-tined fork or the tip of a small knife so steam and moisture can penetrate meat. Rub meat with pepper. Stir gravy mix, wine and orange juice in a deep 3- to 4-quart microwave-safe casserole. Microwave uncovered on high 8 to 10 minutes, stirring twice, until sauce is very thick. Add meat and onions. Cover with a lid. Reduce power to medium and microwave 1 hour. Turn roast over. Add dried fruits and bay leaves. Cover and microwave 1 hour longer, until meat is almost tender when pierced with a fork. Let stand covered 15 minutes, until fork-tender. Transfer roast to a cutting board and let stand 10 minutes before slicing.

Microwave Safety Tips

☐ Avert your face when uncovering a dish; the escaping steam can cause burns. Remove lid or foil from opposite side of dish, *away* from you.

☐ Let liquids, or dishes with a large proportion of liquid in them, stand in the oven a minute or so after cooking. Liquids may become superheated in the microwave yet show no signs of boiling. When moved too soon, liquids could erupt violently.

☐ Fats and sugars attract microwaves, so these parts of a food may become scalding-hot. For example, a jelly doughnut heated in the microwave oven may feel only warm on the outside but the jelly center can be extremely hot. Therefore, allow foods to stand after removal from the microwave so that temperatures equalize.

Perfect Pot Roast

1. Put meat fat-side down in a Dutch oven over medium heat. Cook, turning three or four times, until well browned on all sides, adding oil as needed. Remove meat from Dutch oven; pour off drippings.

2. Put a trivet or a crumbled piece of heavy-duty foil in Dutch oven; place meat on it. Add onion and water and bring to a boil. Reduce heat to low. Cover tightly and simmer 1 hour.

3. Remove meat to a cutting board placed in a jelly-roll pan or other pan with sides to catch juices. Cool 15 to 20 minutes. Cut meat across the grain in ¼-inch-thick slices.

4. Remove trivet or foil from Dutch oven. Return sliced meat to Dutch oven in layers, sprinkling each layer with rosemary, salt and pepper. Add juices from jelly-roll pan and bring to a boil over medium heat. Reduce heat to low. Cover and simmer meat 1½ to 2 hours until fork-tender, spooning juices over it two or three times. Remove from heat.

5. Arrange meat on a heated platter. Cover loosely with foil to keep warm.

6. Skim fat from cooking juices and spoon over meat. Or for a thick gravy, mix flour with 2 to 3 tablespoons cold water in a small bowl until smooth. Bring cooking liquid to a boil; whisk in flour mixture until gravy is thick and smooth. Reduce heat to medium-low and simmer 2 minutes. Spoon over sliced meat and serve.

Makes 12 servings. Per serving (with flour): 300 calories, 28 grams protein, 2 grams carbohydrate, 19 grams fat, 95 milligrams cholesterol, 182 milligrams sodium

Microwave Method: Deeply pierce roast with a two-tined fork or a sharp knife in several places so steam and moisture can penetrate meat. Mix ¼ cup water, 3 tablespoons all-purpose flour and ½ teaspoon gravy browning-and-seasoning sauce in a 4- to 5-quart microwave-safe casserole. Add roast and onion; sprinkle with seasonings. Cover with a lid or vented plastic wrap. Microwave on medium 35 minutes, stirring gravy and rotating dish ¼ turn twice. Turn roast over. Cover and microwave on medium 35 to 40 minutes, stirring gravy and rotating dish twice, until meat is almost tender. Let stand covered 20 to 30 minutes until fork-tender.
Note: The meat is not sliced halfway through cooking in the microwave version.

♥ **LOW-CALORIE**
✳ **MICROWAVE**
Perfect Pot Roast

Every slice is tender and juicy because the meat is sliced midway through cooking. Serve with noodles and green beans.

One 4-pound boneless beef pot roast
    (cross-rib, bottom round, brisket,
    chuck or rump), trimmed of
    excess fat
  1 tablespoon vegetable oil
  1 medium-size onion, sliced
  ½ cup water
  1 teaspoon dried rosemary or
    thyme leaves
  ¾ teaspoon salt
Pepper to taste
1½ tablespoons all-purpose flour
    (optional)

✳ MICROWAVE
Old-fashioned Pot Roast with Vegetables

Serve over egg noodles or with hot biscuits or chunks of good bread. The vegetables cook down considerably during the long baking. All the vegetables except the potato may be cut up ahead of time and kept chilled in a plastic bag.

2 envelopes (¾ ounce each) brown-
    gravy mix
1 cup water
¼ cup red-wine vinegar
One 4-pound lean boneless beef chuck
    cross-rib pot roast, tied, trimmed
    of excess fat
2 medium-size onions, each cut in
    8 wedges
2 medium-size carrots, peeled and cut
    in 1-inch chunks
2 medium-size parsnips, peeled and
    cut in 1-inch chunks
1 large russet potato, scrubbed and cut
    in 1-inch chunks
1 medium-size white turnip, peeled
    and cut in 1-inch chunks
2 stalks celery, cut in 1-inch chunks

1. Heat oven to 325°F.

2. Stir gravy mix, water and vinegar in a Dutch oven until smooth. Place over medium heat and stir until sauce is boiling. Sauce will be very thick. Remove from heat.

3. Add roast to Dutch oven, then pile onions, carrots, parsnips, potato, turnip and celery around meat.

4. Cover pot and transfer to oven. Bake 3 to 3½ hours, until meat and vegetables are tender when pierced with a fork. Remove pot from oven.

5. Uncover and let stand 15 minutes.

6. Transfer roast to a cutting board and remove strings. Cut meat across the grain in ½-inch-thick slices. Place in center of a heated platter. Remove vegetables with a slotted spoon and arrange around meat. Pour gravy into a sauceboat and serve with pot roast.

Makes 6 servings with leftover meat. Per 4-ounce serving meat with ⅙ of the gravy and vegetables: 614 calories, 33 grams protein, 18 grams carbohydrate, 18 grams fat, 118 milligrams cholesterol, 497 milligrams sodium

Microwave Method: Stir gravy mix, water and vinegar in a microwave-safe 1-quart bowl or glass measure. Microwave uncovered on high 8 to 10 minutes, stirring twice, until sauce is very thick. Put 1 tablespoon all-purpose flour into a 20x14-inch oven cooking bag; shake to coat bag. Place in a 13x9-inch microwave-safe baking dish. Scrape in thickened sauce; add roast, then surround with vegetables. Close bag with nylon tie. Cut six ½-inch slits in top of bag. Microwave on medium 2 hours, rotating dish twice, until meat is almost tender when pierced with a fork through a slit in the bag. Let stand in bag 15 minutes until meat is fork-tender. Carefully cut open top of bag. Transfer roast to a cutting board and let stand 10 minutes before slicing.

On the Side

☐ Soothing accompaniments to a hearty pot roast might be creamy mashed or boiled potatoes (see Perfect Mashed Potatoes, page 27 and Buying Potatoes, page 28). Rice is always nice (see Perfect Rice, page 45). And noodles are delicious too—serve them plain, buttered or tossed with a handful of sliced green onions, chopped parsley or a teaspoon of poppy seed. If the roast has a tomato-based sauce, toss noodles with grated Parmesan and a little olive oil for an Italian flair.

☐ Bread is always welcome with a pot roast, to sop up the rich gravy. Try hearty seeded rye, wholesome multigrain bread or thick slices of crusty French bread. A basket of hot biscuits (from your favorite recipe, a mix or a refrigerated roll) or warm corn bread is especially wonderful.

☐ If the pot-roast recipe doesn't include a lot of vegetables, serve one on the side. Buttered carrots, broccoli or Brussel sprouts are good choices. A root vegetable puree, a comforting go-with, is easy to make. Simmer peeled rutabaga or turnip chunks with carrots and peeled potatoes until tender. Drain and mash in the pot or whirl in a food processor. Add a little milk or sour cream and season with salt and pepper.

Pot Roast with White Beans and Tomato

The amount of garlic may seem excessive, but long, slow cooking mellows the flavor.

One 4-pound lean boneless beef chuck
    cross-rib pot roast, tied, trimmed
    of excess fat
½ teaspoon pepper
2 envelopes (¾ ounce each) brown-
    gravy mix
1 cup water
2 cups frozen or fresh chopped onions
3 large cloves garlic, cut in thin slivers
    (about 2 tablespoons)
½ teaspoon dried thyme leaves, crumbled
1 can (19 ounces) cannellini or other
    small white beans, such as navy
    beans, rinsed and drained
1 cup canned crushed tomatoes in
    purée

1. Heat oven to 325°F.

2. Rub meat all over with pepper.

3. Stir gravy mix and water in a Dutch oven until smooth. Add onions, garlic and thyme. Stir over medium heat until boiling. Sauce will be very thick. Remove from heat and add meat to Dutch oven.

4. Transfer pot to oven, cover and bake 3 hours. Stir in beans and tomatoes.

5. Bake uncovered 20 to 30 minutes longer, until meat is fork-tender. Remove pot from oven and let stand 15 minutes.

6. Transfer roast to a cutting board and remove strings. Cut meat across the grain in ½-inch-thick slices. Arrange on a heated platter. Spoon some sauce on top; serve remaining sauce and beans on the side.

Makes 6 servings with leftover meat. Per 4-ounce serving meat with ⅙ of the bean sauce: 645 calories, 37 grams protein, 22 grams carbohydrate, 18 grams fat, 118 milligrams cholesterol, 525 milligrams sodium

Microwave Method: Reduce amount of pepper to ¼ teaspoon. Deeply pierce roast all over with a two-tined fork or the tip of a small knife so steam and moisture can penetrate meat; rub with pepper. Stir gravy mix and water in a deep 3- to 4-quart microwave-safe casserole; add onions, garlic and thyme. Microwave uncovered on high 10 to 12 minutes, until sauce is very thick, stirring twice. Add roast and cover with a lid. Reduce power to medium; microwave 1 hour.

Turn roast over. Cover and microwave 45 minutes. Stir in beans and tomatoes. Cover and continue to microwave 15 minutes longer, until meat is almost tender when pierced with a fork. Remove from oven. Let stand covered 15 minutes or until meat is fork-tender. Transfer roast to a cutting board and let stand 10 minutes before slicing.

French Pot Roast

For a thicker sauce, stir a mixture of 3 tablespoons all-purpose flour and ¼ cup water into the pan juices and simmer until thick.

2 tablespoons vegetable oil
One 3- to 4-pound boneless beef chuck
    cross-rib pot roast, tied, trimmed
    of excess fat
1½ cups thinly sliced leeks, rinsed well
    to remove grit
¾ cup chopped carrots
¾ cup diced celery with leaves
1 teaspoon minced fresh garlic
1 cup dry red wine or ¾ cup beef
    broth and 2 tablespoons red-wine
    vinegar
1 teaspoon salt
½ teaspoon pepper
½ teaspoon dried thyme leaves
Two 2-inch-long bay leaves

1. Heat oven to 325°F.

2. Pat meat dry with paper towels.

3. Heat oil over medium heat in a Dutch oven or a large ovenproof pot until hot but not smoking. Add roast, leeks, carrots, celery and garlic to Dutch oven. Cook roast until browned on all sides; stir vegetables occasionally.

4. Add wine, salt, pepper, thyme and bay leaves to Dutch oven and bring to a boil.

5. Cover tightly and transfer pot to oven. Bake 2½ to 3 hours, until meat is tender when pierced with a fork.

6. Transfer meat to a cutting board. Cover loosely with a foil tent to keep warm. Let stand 10 to 15 minutes.

7. Discard bay leaves and skim fat from sauce. Remove strings from roast and cut across the grain in thin slices. Arrange on a heated platter; spoon sauce over meat and serve.

Makes 8 servings. Per serving: 334 calories, 34 grams protein, 7 grams carbohydrate, 18 grams fat, 111 milligrams cholesterol, 425 milligrams sodium

First-Up-in-the-Morning Braised Pot Roast

Serve this succulent onion-enriched pot roast with buttered asparagus spears and baked potatoes. In the family that created this dish, the first person up on Sunday puts it in the oven so it will be ready for dinner at midday.

One 5½-pound boneless beef round or
rump roast, trimmed of excess fat
1 teaspoon salt
½ teaspoon pepper, or to taste
½ teaspoon garlic powder
4 tablespoons vegetable oil
2 pounds onions, thinly sliced
1 cup water
3 beef bouillon cubes

1. Heat oven to 300°F.

2. Pat meat dry with paper towels. Season with salt, pepper and garlic powder.

3. Heat 3 tablespoons of the oil in a Dutch oven or a large heavy pot over medium heat until hot but not smoking. Add meat and brown well on all sides. Remove meat to a plate.

4. Add remaining 1 tablespoon oil to Dutch oven. Stir in onions. Cook about 10 minutes, stirring occasionally, until onions are lightly browned and start to soften.

5. Return meat to Dutch oven. Spoon some of the onions over top. Add water and bouillon cubes. Raise heat to high. Cover and bring liquid to a boil.

6. Transfer pot to oven. Bake about 3½ hours, until meat is tender when pierced with a fork. Remove from oven. Uncover and let stand 10 minutes.

7. Remove meat to a cutting board and cut against the grain in thin slices. Arrange on a heated platter and top with the onions. Put pan juices in a sauceboat to pass on the side.

Makes 10 servings. Per serving: 363 calories, 48 grams protein, 8 grams carbohydrate, 15 grams fat, 135 milligrams cholesterol, 623 milligrams sodium

First-Up-in-the-Morning Braised Rump Roast

Busy-Day Pot Roast

♥ LOW-CALORIE
Busy-Day Pot Roast

This recipe is assembled in less than 5 minutes—there are only four ingredients—and bakes unattended while you tend to other things. Serve with rice and a combination of steamed broccoli and quartered mushrooms sprinkled with crushed red-pepper flakes.

One 3- to 4-pound boneless beef chuck
     cross-rib pot roast, tied, trimmed
     of excess fat
1 can (10¾ ounces) cream of
     mushroom soup, undiluted
1 envelope (from a 2.75-ounce
     package) onion-soup mix
1 tablespoon bottled steak sauce

1. Heat oven to 325°F.

2. Put meat in a Dutch oven. Mix remaining ingredients in a small bowl. Spread over top and sides of roast.

3. Cover and bake about 3 hours, until meat is tender when pierced with a fork. Remove from oven.

4. Transfer meat to a cutting board. Let stand about 5 minutes. Remove strings. Cut across the grain in thin slices and arrange on a heated platter. Pour gravy into a sauceboat to pass on the side.

Makes 8 to 10 servings. Per 3½-ounce serving with 3 tablespoons gravy: 267 calories, 20 grams protein, 4 grams carbohydrate, 19 grams fat, 76 milligrams cholesterol, 544 milligrams sodium

20

Hungarian Pot Roast with Vegetables

A one-skillet main dish. Top servings with sour cream or yogurt and serve with a good rye bread to soak up the delicious juices.

One 1½-pound boneless beef chuck
    steak, 1½-inches thick, trimmed
    of excess fat and cut in 4 pieces
1 tablespoon all-purpose flour mixed
    with ¾ teaspoon salt
2 tablespoons vegetable oil
1 large onion, coarsely chopped (about
    1 cup)
½ teaspoon minced fresh garlic
1 tablespoon paprika
½ teaspoon caraway seed
2 to 3 cups water
3 medium-size all-purpose potatoes,
    peeled if desired, cut in ½-inch
    chunks (about 2 cups)
1 medium-size green bell pepper, cut
    in ½-inch chunks (about 1 cup)
1 large ripe fresh tomato, diced

1. Pound each piece of meat with a meat mallet or the bottom of a heavy skillet until ¼-inch thick. Coat meat with flour mixture.

2. Heat oil in a large heavy skillet over medium-high heat until hot but not smoking. Add meat and brown on both sides. Remove meat to a plate.

3. Add onion and garlic to skillet. Cook, stirring often, until lightly browned. Stir in paprika and caraway seed, then 2 cups of the water.

4. Return meat to skillet in a single layer. Bring liquid to a boil; reduce heat to low. Cover and simmer 1 hour, turning once and adding up to 1 more cup water if sauce seems dry, until meat is almost tender when pierced with a fork.

5. Add potatoes and bell pepper to skillet. Increase heat to medium and bring liquid to a simmer. Reduce heat to low. Cover and simmer 20 to 30 minutes longer, until meat and vegetables are tender.

6. Add tomato and cook 1 minute, just until thoroughly heated.

7. Arrange meat, vegetables and sauce on dinner plates and serve.

Makes 4 servings. Per serving: 574 calories, 22 grams protein, 25 grams carbohydrate, 43 grams fat, 77 milligrams cholesterol, 475 milligrams sodium

Freezing Meat

☐ Meat is expensive, so before you freeze it, wrap it carefully to protect your investment from freezer burn or moisture loss. Wrap the meat in freezer paper (shiny side in), then in foil. Or wrap the meat in a plastic freezer bag after expelling the air. Label it clearly with the contents and the date. If you are freezing several packages at once, spread them out until they are solidly frozen. The meat should freeze as quickly as possible; a slow freeze allows the cells to expand and rupture, so when you thaw the meat it will lose half its juices. A freezer should maintain a constant temperature of 0°F or lower to keep frozen foods in top condition.

☐ Do not unwrap frozen meat or poultry that you buy for storage in your own freezer. The packages have been vacuum-packed or heat-sealed for efficient freezing. Simply wrap the package with foil, label and freeze.

☐ It is better not to refreeze meat that has partially or completely defrosted. There is nothing dangerous about refrozen meat, but the loss of juices will leave the meat dry and tasteless.

☐ To defrost meat: Loosen package wrappings and leave it in the refrigerator for about 24 hours. Never leave meat out on the kitchen counter to defrost. When meat thaws at room temperature, all the juices run out.

☐ Buying meat on sale for freezing is a good way to help the budget, but only if the meat fits your menu needs. Check the meat to see how much waste there is in fat and bone; you are not saving money if you have to throw out a good portion of what you buy. And of course, think about the space available in your freezer.

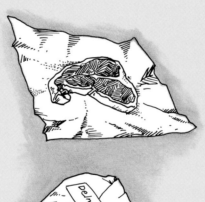

Sauerbraten with Sweet-Sour Gravy

Gingersnaps thicken and flavor the sauce of this traditional German specialty. Crush them in a food processor or a blender or put them in a plastic bag and crush with a rolling pin.

One 3½-pound lean boneless beef
    chuck cross-rib or shoulder pot
    roast, tied, trimmed of excess fat
2 tablespoons vegetable oil
1½ cups cranberry juice or beef broth
1 can (10¾ ounces) condensed
    cream of chicken or celery soup,
    undiluted
1 can (8 ounces) tomato sauce
1 medium-size onion, finely chopped
    (about ½ cup)
¼ cup cider vinegar
½ teaspoon ground ginger
½ teaspoon pepper
¼ teaspoon ground cloves
One 1-inch-long bay leaf
½ cup raisins
5 gingersnap cookies, finely crushed
    (about ¼ cup)

1. Pat meat dry with paper towels.

2. Heat oil in a Dutch oven over medium-high heat until hot but not smoking. Add meat and turn to brown on all sides.

3. Add cranberry juice, soup, tomato sauce, onion, vinegar, ginger, pepper, cloves and bay leaf to Dutch oven. Stir to mix well. Bring to a boil. Reduce heat to low. Cover and simmer 2 hours.

4. Add raisins. Cover and simmer 1 hour longer, until meat is tender when pierced with a fork. Remove from heat.

5. Transfer roast to a cutting board. Let stand while making sauce.

6. Discard bay leaf. Skim excess fat from surface of pan juices. Add cookie crumbs and simmer, stirring constantly, until crumbs are dissolved and the sauce thickens.

7. Remove strings from roast. Cut meat across the grain in thin slices. Arrange on a heated platter. Spoon some of the sauce over meat; pour the rest into a sauceboat to pass on the side.

Makes 8 servings plus leftovers. Per 4-ounce serving with ½ cup sauce: 606 calories, 30 grams protein, 32 grams carbohydrate, 40 grams fat, 113 milligrams cholesterol, 753 milligrams sodium

Microwave Method: Omit the vegetable oil. Reduce the amount of cranberry juice or broth to 1 cup. Reduce the amount of pepper to ¼ teaspoon. Deeply pierce roast all over with a two-tined fork or the tip of a small knife so steam and moisture can penetrate meat. Stir cranberry juice, soup, tomato sauce, onion, vinegar, ginger, pepper, cloves and bay leaf in a deep 3- to 4-quart microwave-safe casserole. Microwave uncovered on high 8 to 10 minutes, stirring twice, until liquid is simmering. Add meat and cover with a lid. Reduce power to medium and microwave 1 hour. Turn roast over and add raisins. Cover and continue to microwave on medium 1 hour, until meat is almost tender when pierced with a fork. Let stand covered 15 minutes, until fork-tender. Transfer roast to a cutting board. Skim off fat and stir cookie crumbs into sauce. Microwave on high 1½ to 2 minutes to thicken. Proceed as directed.

Perfect Baked Potatoes

☐ The best potatoes for baking are russet potatoes. Their dry flaky texture makes them the perfect foil for butter, sour cream or rich sauces and meat gravies.

☐ To bake: Heat the oven to 400°F. Scrub one large (or two small) potatoes per person. Bake directly on the oven rack or in a baking pan 45 to 55 minutes, until potatoes feel soft when gently squeezed (wear an oven mitt when testing) or are tender when pierced with a fork.

☐ Remove from oven; cut a slit in the top and serve with butter or margarine, sour cream or plain yogurt and salt and pepper. A small dish of snipped fresh chives or sliced green onions is an excellent addition.

☐ Never bake potatoes wrapped in foil; they will steam rather than bake.

☐ To keep baked potatoes warm: Leave them in a turned-off oven for up to 20 minutes, until ready to serve.

☐ To bake potatoes in the microwave: Pierce each potato in several places with a fork. Place in microwave oven on a plastic rack or paper towel. If baking four potatoes, microwave on high 10 to 12 minutes (if baking only one, microwave about 6 minutes), turning once, until potatoes feel soft near the skin but still a bit firm in the center. Remove from oven and let stand 5 minutes to complete cooking.

Beef and Vegetables "Pot" Roast

Try this oven-bag method for other large cuts of meat as well.

- **1 tablespoon all-purpose flour**
- **One 3-pound lean boneless beef chuck cross-rib or shoulder pot roast, tied, trimmed of excess fat**
- **1 teaspoon vegetable oil**
- **½ teaspoon salt**
- **¼ teaspoon pepper**
- **Paprika**
- **1 can (8 ounces) tomato sauce**
- **½ cup water**
- **1 package (1.9 ounces) French onion-soup mix**
- **1 teaspoon minced fresh garlic**
- **1 teaspoon dried marjoram or oregano leaves, crumbled**
- **3 medium-size all-purpose potatoes (about 1 pound), scrubbed and halved crosswise**
- **3 medium-size carrots, cut in 1-inch chunks**
- **3 medium-size stalks celery, quartered crosswise**

1. Heat oven to 325°F. Put flour into a 20 x 14-inch oven cooking bag with nylon tie and shake to coat bag. Place bag in a 13x9-inch baking dish.

2. Rub roast all over with oil. Season with salt and pepper and sprinkle with paprika.

3. Roll down top of bag and add tomato sauce, water, soup mix, garlic and marjoram. Squeeze bag gently to mix. Add roast, then surround with vegetables. Close bag. Make six ½-inch slits in top of bag.

4. Bake 2 to 2½ hours, until meat and vegetables are tender when pierced with a fork through a slit in the bag. Remove from oven and let stand in bag 15 minutes.

5. Carefully cut open top of bag. Transfer roast to a cutting board. Remove strings and let stand 10 minutes.

6. Cut meat across the grain in ½-inch-thick slices. Arrange on a heated platter. Remove vegetables to platter with a large spoon. Skim fat from gravy in bag; spoon gravy over meat and vegetables and serve.

Makes 4 servings with leftovers. Per 4-ounce serving meat with ¼ cup gravy and ¼ of the vegetables: 458 calories, 39 grams protein, 34 grams carbohydrate, 18 grams fat, 120 milligrams cholesterol, 1,770 milligrams sodium

Beef and Vegetables "Pot" Roast

Microwave Classic Pot Roast

✳ MICROWAVE
Microwave Classic Pot Roast

One 3-pound boneless beef chuck roast,
    trimmed of excess fat
2 medium-size onions, each cut in
    8 wedges
½ cup water or beef broth
1 teaspoon salt
¼ teaspoon pepper
One 2-inch-long bay leaf
2 tablespoons all-purpose flour
6 medium-size carrots, cut in
    1-inch pieces
4 medium-size all-purpose potatoes,
    each cut in 8 chunks (about 4
    cups)
2 stalks celery, cut in 1-inch pieces
    (about 1½ cups)

1. Deeply pierce roast all over with a two-tined fork or a sharp knife so steam and moisture can penetrate meat. Place roast in a 4- to 5-quart microwave-safe casserole. Add half of the onions, the water, salt, pepper and bay leaf.

2. Cover with a lid or vented plastic wrap. Microwave on medium 30 minutes, rotating dish ¼ turn twice.

3. Turn roast over and stir flour into pan juices. Scatter carrots, potatoes and celery around roast.

4. Cover and microwave on medium 35 to 40 minutes, rotating dish ¼ turn and stirring vegetables twice, until meat and vegetables are almost tender. Remove from oven. Let stand covered 20 to 30 minutes, until meat and vegetables are fork-tender.

5. Discard bay leaf. Transfer roast to a cutting board and cut across the grain in thin slices. Arrange meat and vegetables on a heated platter. Spoon the pan juices over meat and serve.

Makes 6 servings. Per serving: 615 calories, 47 grams protein, 25 grams carbohydrate, 35 grams fat, 154 milligrams cholesterol, 565 milligrams sodium

Note: For a thicker gravy, mix 1 tablespoon all-purpose flour with 2 tablespoons water in a cup until smooth. Stir into juices left in casserole after removing meat and vegetables and microwave 2 to 3 minutes, until bubbly and thickened.

Pot Roast Twice

One of the best things about pot roast, besides the fabulous taste and the wonderful aroma, is that there is usually some left over for another meal. You can always reheat the roast in the gravy, but if you are looking for something different, try these ideas and the recipes that follow.

Steak and Eggs: Quickly fry meat slices in a nonstick skillet in a small amount of oil or butter. Break an egg over each slice. Cover and cook over low heat until eggs are done the way you like them. Good with warm chili sauce and French fries.

Stir-fry: Cut meat in strips. Add meat and frozen Chinese-style vegetables to hot oil in a wok or a large skillet. Season with soy sauce, garlic and ginger. Cook, stirring constantly, until vegetables are crisp-tender. Sprinkle with chopped fresh cilantro or sliced green onions. Serve over rice or Chinese noodles.

Pot-Roast Melt: Spread rye bread with mustard; top with sliced meat, tomatoes, Swiss cheese and red onion. Place under broiler to melt cheese. Serve with potato chips and pickles.

Spinach Chef's Salad: Wash and dry fresh spinach; add strips of cold meat, drained canned chick-peas, cheese cubes, roasted red peppers and sliced fresh mushrooms. Toss with bottled Italian dressing.

Tacos: Tear meat in shreds, sprinkle with taco-seasoning mix, and heat with canned crushed tomatoes. Spoon into taco shells; top with sour cream, shredded lettuce, Cheddar or Monterey Jack cheese, diced jalapeño peppers, chopped avocado and onions.

⏱ **MAKE-AHEAD**
Dilled Sour-Cream Sauce

Good with cold or hot sliced pot roast.

½ cup sour cream
½ cup mayonnaise
3 tablespoons tomato ketchup
2 tablespoons chopped fresh dill

1. Mix all ingredients in small bowl. Cover; refrigerate up to 1 week, until ready to serve.

Makes 1 cup. Per 2 tablespoons: 57 calories, 0 grams protein, 1 gram carbohydrate, 6 grams fat, 6 milligrams cholesterol, 64 milligrams sodium

⏱ **MAKE-AHEAD**
Horseradish Sauce

Serve with cold sliced pot roast.

¾ cup sour cream
¼ cup chopped radishes
¼ cup sliced green onions
4 teaspoons prepared white horseradish
¼ teaspoon Worcestershire sauce
¼ teaspoon salt
Pepper to taste

1. Mix all ingredients in a small bowl. Cover and refrigerate up to 2 days, until ready to serve.

Makes 1 cup. Per tablespoon: 25 calories, 0 grams protein, 1 gram carbohydrate, 2 grams fat, 5 milligrams cholesterol, 42 milligrams sodium

Herbed Mushroom Topping

For a quick stew, heat diced pot roast in gravy and add this topping. Serve over rice.

10 ounces mushrooms
2 tablespoons butter or margarine
¼ teaspoon dried thyme leaves
¼ teaspoon salt
¼ teaspoon pepper
1 tablespoon grated Parmesan cheese
1 tablespoon chopped fresh parsley

1. Slice 4 mushrooms; chop remainder.

2. Melt butter in a medium-size nonstick skillet over medium heat. Add mushrooms and thyme. Cook 6 to 7 minutes, stirring frequently, until mushrooms release their liquid. Add remaining ingredients. Serve hot.

Makes about 1 cup, 4 servings. Per serving: 76 calories, 2 grams protein, 4 grams carbohydrate, 6 grams fat, 16 milligrams cholesterol with butter, 8 milligrams cholesterol with margarine, 440 milligrams sodium

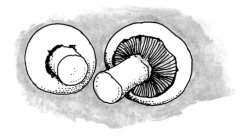

Beef-and-Potato Hash

♥ LOW-CALORIE
Beef-and-Potato Hash

You can make this savory hash with any leftover pot roast, or with roast beef from the deli counter. Serve it with a crisp green salad.

12 ounces well-trimmed leftover pot roast, finely diced (about 2 cups)
 1 large onion, halved and thinly sliced
 3 patties (3 ounces each) frozen shredded hash browns, thawed and broken in small pieces
 1 jar (7 ounces) roasted red peppers, drained and chopped
½ teaspoon dry mustard
½ teaspoon salt
½ teaspoon pepper
 2 tablespoons olive oil
 2 tablespoons butter or margarine

1. Mix pot roast, onion, hash browns, roasted peppers, mustard, salt and pepper in a large bowl.

2. Heat oil and butter in a large nonstick skillet over medium heat. When butter is foamy, add hash mixture. Press down into a flat round with a wide spatula to cover bottom of skillet.

3. Cook, without stirring, 10 minutes, until bottom is browned and crisp, pressing occasionally. Turn hash in clumps and press back into a round. Cook 10 minutes longer, without stirring, until bottom is browned and crisp. Remove from heat.

4. Loosen hash with a spatula. Invert onto a heated round platter. Serve immediately.

Makes 6 servings. Per serving: 249 calories, 18 grams protein, 12 grams carbohydrate, 14 grams fat, 64 milligrams cholesterol with butter, 52 milligrams cholesterol with margarine, 268 milligrams sodium

Brisket

Brisket, the breast portion of the animal, is a long, flat piece of meat sold whole or in pieces: the flat (or first) cut, the middle cut and the point cut. The flat cut is the thinnest; it is also the leanest and the easiest to slice. Brisket is sold fresh or pickled in a spiced brine and called corned beef. It is a flavorful cut but needs long, slow, even, moist cooking to make it tender. To test for doneness: Insert a two-tined meat fork in the thickest part; meat should offer no resistance. However, brisket should not be cooked until it falls apart.

Brisket is a little tricky to carve. Look to see which way the fibers (the grain) run through the meat. It will vary; whichever way it runs, cut across it on a slight angle. The thicker point cut can be sliced in the same way, or you may cut off the top layer of meat, remove the fat running between the two pieces and slice each piece separately.

🕐 **MAKE-AHEAD**
♥ **LOW-CALORIE**

Brisket with Cranberry-Tomato Gravy

A super easy brisket with lots of hearty gravy.

One 5-pound beef brisket, trimmed of
    surface fat
2 tablespoons vegetable oil
3 medium-size onions, finely chopped
1 can (16 ounces) whole-berry
    cranberry sauce
1 can (15 ounces) tomato sauce

1. Pat meat dry with paper towels.

2. Heat oil in a large heavy pot or a Dutch oven over medium-high heat until hot but not smoking. Add brisket and brown on all sides. Remove to a sheet of foil or a large platter.

3. Add onions, cranberry sauce and tomato sauce to pot and stir to blend. Return brisket to pot. Cover tightly and bring liquid to a boil. Reduce heat to low and simmer 2½ to 3 hours, until meat is tender when pierced with a fork. (Can be made ahead to this point and refrigerated up to 2 days; see Note.)

4. Remove brisket to a cutting board and cover loosely with a foil tent to keep warm.

5. Uncover pot and simmer gravy about 10 minutes, stirring frequently, until thickened. Remove from heat. Skim fat from surface and pour into a sauceboat.

6. Cut brisket on an angle across the grain in thin slices. Arrange on a heated platter. Spoon a little of the gravy over meat; pass the remaining gravy on the side.

Makes 10 servings. Per serving: 300 calories, 29 grams protein, 22 grams carbohydrate, 8 grams fat, 84 milligrams cholesterol, 368 milligrams sodium

Note: To reheat brisket: Skim fat from surface of gravy. Cook, covered, over medium-low heat 30 minutes, until meat and gravy are hot. Continue as directed.

Perfect Mashed Potatoes

A bowl of creamy mashed potatoes is a perfect complement to a hearty, fragrant pot roast or brisket. With or without lumps, skins on or off, mashed potatoes are a sure pleaser.

☐ Peel or scrub, if you prefer the skins on, one medium-size russet or all-purpose potato for each serving. Cut potatoes in quarters and cook covered in a saucepan of salted simmering water until very tender. Drain in a colander. Return potatoes to the cooking pot and shake over medium-low heat for a few minutes to dry potatoes completely. Mash in the cooking pot with a potato masher, or beat on low speed with a portable electric mixer, or press through a potato ricer or through a strainer with the back of a wooden spoon. While mashing, add enough warm milk or cream and bits of butter or margarine to bring the potatoes to the desired texture. Sour cream or plain yogurt is delicious too. Season the potatoes with salt and pepper and serve hot. Mashed potatoes may be prepared ahead and chilled. Reheat in a covered baking dish in a 350°F oven about 20 minutes, until hot.

☐ You can vary the flavor of mashed potatoes several ways: Top them with browned sliced onions or shallots; stir in sliced green onions or snipped chives; or add a fresh flavor by seasoning the mashed potatoes with chopped parsley and a squeeze of lemon juice. Garlic lovers can simmer the potatoes in chicken broth along with 2 or 3 garlic cloves, then mash the garlic with the potatoes. Or simmer carrots, parsnips or turnips with the potatoes to make a root-vegetable purée. For a green-vegetable purée, add a box of frozen chopped broccoli or spinach to simmering potatoes about 5 minutes before they're done. Season with a touch of ground nutmeg.

Texas-Style Beef Brisket

Serve with Skinny Fries (recipe follows) or frozen fries, crisp cole slaw and hot corn bread.

One 4-pound flat-cut beef brisket,
    trimmed of surface fat
2 tablespoons chili powder
2 medium-size onions, each cut in
    8 wedges
4 ounces bacon (4 thick or 6 regular
    slices), cut in 1-inch pieces
1 cup bottled barbecue sauce
1 can (6 ounces) tomato paste
3 beef bouillon cubes or 3 teaspoons
    instant broth granules

1. Heat oven to 450°F. Grease a 13x9-inch baking pan.

2. Rub brisket all over with chili powder. Place in prepared pan. Scatter onions and bacon around meat.

3. Bake 20 minutes, until brisket and bacon are lightly browned. Remove from oven.

4. Remove accumulated fat from baking pan with a bulb baster or a large spoon and discard.

5. Meanwhile, mix barbecue sauce, tomato paste and bouillon in a small saucepan. Bring to a boil over medium heat, stirring to dissolve bouillon cubes.

6. Drizzle hot sauce into pan around meat. With a wooden spoon, stir to mix with onions and bacon. Cover baking pan with foil; turn back one corner of foil 2 inches.

7. Return pan to oven. Reduce oven temperature to 325°F. Bake brisket 3 to 3½ hours, until meat is fork-tender. Remove from oven.

8. Remove brisket to a cutting board. Let stand 15 minutes.

9. Cut brisket on an angle across the grain in ½-inch-thick slices. Arrange on a heated platter. Pour sauce into a sauceboat and spoon off fat. Serve brisket, passing sauce on the side.

Makes 8 servings meat and 3 cups sauce. Per serving with ¼ cup sauce: 438 calories, 38 grams protein, 6 grams carbohydrate, 28 grams fat, 123 milligrams cholesterol, 595 milligrams sodium

♥ LOW-CALORIE

Skinny Fries

Just as crispy and delicious as fries cooked in deep fat, but without the extra calories.

1¼ pounds russet potatoes, scrubbed
    and cut in thin matchstick strips
    (about 4 cups)
1 tablespoon vegetable oil
¼ teaspoon salt
¼ teaspoon pepper

1. Place one oven rack in top third of the oven and another in the middle. Heat oven to 450°F. Lightly coat two 15½x10½-inch jelly-roll pans or cookie sheets with no-stick vegetable cooking spray.

2. Put half of the potatoes, oil, salt and pepper in each prepared pan. Mix with hands and arrange potato strips in a single layer.

3. Bake 12 to 15 minutes, until bottoms of potatoes start to brown. Remove from oven and turn potatoes over.

4. Return potatoes to oven, reversing pans on oven racks. Bake 8 to 12 minutes, until potatoes are crisp and browned. If some potatoes cook faster than others, remove them from pans as they brown. Remove potatoes from oven and transfer immediately to a serving dish. Serve hot.

Makes 4 servings. Per serving: 111 calories, 2 grams protein, 18 grams carbohydrate, 3 grams fat, 0 milligrams cholesterol, 136 milligrams sodium

---

Buying Potatoes

Choose fairly clean, smooth, firm potatoes. For even cooking, pick potatoes that are about the same size. Select regular shapes to save on waste in peeling. Reject wilted potatoes or those with wrinkled skins, soft dark spots, cut surfaces or green skins. Green spots under the skin of the potatoes may mean they were exposed to light; cut the spots off before cooking to eliminate bitterness.

Foil-Baked Beef Brisket with Potatoes and Whole Onions

The potatoes and the onions are baked directly on the oven rack. A delicious accompaniment is Horseradish Sauce (recipe, page 25). A spinach and mushroom salad with Italian dressing and baked apples or apple pie will complete the meal.

One 2-pound beef brisket, trimmed of surface fat
¼ teaspoon coarsely ground black pepper
½ envelope onion-mushroom soup mix (about 2½ tablespoons)
4 large carrots, well scrubbed
One 2-inch-long bay leaf
4 russet potatoes (about 6 ounces each), well scrubbed
4 large yellow onions (about 8 ounces each), not peeled, but washed, dried and rubbed with vegetable oil

1. Heat oven to 400°F. Tear off a strip of heavy-duty foil large enough to enclose meat and carrots. Have ready a shallow baking pan just large enough to hold foil package.

2. Place brisket in center of foil. Sprinkle with pepper and soup mix. Top with carrots and bay leaf.

3. Bring up sides and ends of foil; fold edges over a few times to seal. Place packet in baking pan.

4. Bake brisket 1½ hours. Place potatoes and onions directly on oven rack. Bake 45 minutes, until brisket is tender when pierced with a fork inserted through the foil and potatoes and onions are soft when gently squeezed. Remove from oven and let stand 10 minutes.

5. Open foil slowly, being careful to avoid any rush of steam. Discard bay leaf and transfer brisket to a cutting board and carrots to a heated serving platter. Carefully pour pan juices into a sauceboat and skim off fat.

6. Cut meat on an angle across the grain in thin slices. Arrange on platter. Cut off root ends of onions and gently squeeze each until pulp pops out. Discard skins and arrange onions and potatoes on platter. Serve, passing pan juices on the side.

Makes 4 servings. Per serving: 720 calories, 45 grams protein, 54 grams carbohydrate, 35 grams fat, 152 milligrams cholesterol, 660 milligrams sodium

Variation: You can substitute a 3-pound rump roast for the brisket. Proceed as directed, increasing the amount of soup mix to 4 tablespoons and the total baking time to 2½ hours.

Garnishes

To make a platter of sliced meat look special, garnish with sprigs or leaves of fresh herbs, or sprinkle with snipped or chopped herbs. Chopped parsley or dill add sparkle. Snipped chives or green onions add color and a burst of flavor. Mexican-inspired dishes benefit from chopped fresh cilantro. Sprigs of watercress or tender leaves of Boston or red-leaf lettuce add an elegant touch to a roast.

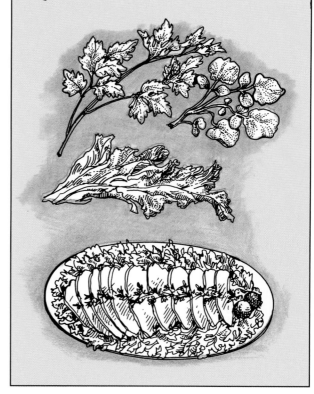

Onion-Smothered Beef Brisket

You can cook, slice and refrigerate the brisket the day before, then reheat as directed when you're ready to serve.

- **3 large onions, halved and thinly sliced (about 3 cups)**
- **One 4-pound flat-cut beef brisket, top fat trimmed to ¼ inch**
- **1 large clove garlic, cut in half**
- **2 teaspoons paprika**
- **¼ teaspoon pepper**
- **1½ cups beef broth**

1. Heat oven to 350°F.

2. Put onions in the center of a large roasting pan. Rub brisket with garlic, then add garlic clove to onions. Sprinkle brisket with paprika and pepper. Place brisket fat-side up on onions. Pour in broth. Cover pan with foil.

3. Bake 2½ hours, until meat is almost tender when pierced with a fork. Remove foil and bake 30 minutes longer, until meat is tender and top is golden brown.

4. Remove meat to a cutting board. Cover loosely with foil and let stand 10 minutes.

5. Cut meat on an angle across the grain in thin slices. Arrange on a heated platter. Skim fat from pan juices. Spoon onions and juices over meat and serve.

To refrigerate before serving: Return sliced meat to pan with juices and onions; cover and refrigerate for a day. To serve: Heat in 350°F oven 30 to 35 minutes, until hot.

Makes 8 servings. Per serving: 284 calories, 32 grams protein, 4 grams carbohydrate, 15 grams fat, 100 milligrams cholesterol, 185 milligrams sodium

Microwave Method: Put onions in a 4-quart microwave-safe baking dish. Pierce brisket in several places with a two-tined fork or the tip of a small knife so steam and moisture can penetrate meat. Season, then place on onions fat-side down; pour in ¾ cup beef broth. Cover with a lid or vented plastic wrap and microwave on medium 1 hour. Rotate dish ¼ turn; turn meat over. Cover and microwave 30 to 45 minutes longer, rotating dish ¼ turn once, until brisket is almost tender. Let stand covered 20 to 30 minutes, until fork-tender. Continue as directed.

Corned-Beef Dinner

Serve with prepared horseradish and mustard. The cooking liquid makes a flavorful base for split-pea soup. Slice only what you need and refrigerate the remaining meat in the cooking liquid to keep it moist.

- **One 5-pound corned-beef brisket, trimmed of surface fat**
- **2 medium-size onions, each studded with 5 whole cloves**
- **2 large stalks celery, halved**
- **Water**
- **8 small thin-skinned potatoes, peeled**
- **4 small white turnips, peeled**
- **1 small head cabbage, cut in wedges**
- **4 large carrots, cut in chunks**

1. Place corned beef, onions and celery in a large Dutch oven. Add enough water to cover meat and vegetables. Bring to a boil over high heat. Skim off the foam that rises to the surface.

2. Reduce heat to low. Cover and simmer about 3 hours, until corned beef is tender when pierced with a fork.

3. Discard onions and celery. Add remaining vegetables to Dutch oven. Raise heat to medium-high and return liquid to a boil. Reduce heat to low. Cover and simmer 30 minutes, until vegetables are tender.

4. Remove meat to a cutting board and cut on an angle across the grain in thin slices. Arrange on a heated platter. Remove vegetables from Dutch oven with a slotted spoon, arrange around meat and serve.

Makes 4 servings with leftover meat. Per 4-ounce serving meat with vegetables: 569 calories, 38 grams protein, 32 grams carbohydrate, 35 grams fat, 106 milligrams cholesterol, 1,164 milligrams sodium

Barbecue-Style Microwave Brisket

✳ MICROWAVE
Barbecue-Style Microwave Brisket

Cut down on cooking time and avoid heating up your kitchen by making this favorite in your microwave.

One 3-pound flat-cut beef brisket, top fat trimmed to ¼ inch
2 teaspoons garlic powder
⅔ cup bottled barbecue sauce

1. Pierce brisket in several places with a two-tined fork or the tip of a small knife so steam and moisture can penetrate meat. Season both sides with garlic powder. Place brisket fat-side down in a 13x9-inch microwave-safe baking dish. Cover with vented plastic wrap.

2. Microwave brisket on medium 45 minutes, rotating dish ¼ turn twice.

3. Turn meat; pour barbecue sauce over top. Cover with vented plastic wrap.

4. Microwave on medium 40 to 45 minutes longer, rotating dish ¼ turn once, until brisket is almost tender when pierced with a fork. Remove from oven. Let stand covered 20 to 25 minutes, until meat is fork-tender.

5. Transfer brisket to a cutting board. Cut on an angle across the grain in thin slices. Arrange on a heated platter. Spoon pan juices over the top and serve.

Makes 8 servings. Per serving: 362 calories, 20 grams protein, 2 grams carbohydrate, 30 grams fat, 77 milligrams cholesterol, 237 milligrams sodium

Ribs

Whether you grill these ribs in the backyard or at home on the range, they're delicious. Because the temperature, the wind and the type of grill affect cooking time outdoors, check for doneness often rather than relying on the clock.

Texas-Style Barbecued Beef Ribs

Place your grill in a protected area so gusts of wind won't smoke out your party. Serve with potato salad—try the award-winning recipe that follows.

> 2 tablespoons butter or margarine
> ¼ cup finely chopped onion
> 1 large clove garlic, minced
> ½ cup tomato ketchup
> ½ cup cider vinegar
> ½ cup water
> 2 tablespoons granulated sugar
> 1 tablespoon Worcestershire sauce
> One 1-inch-long bay leaf, crushed
> 2 teaspoons dry mustard
> 2 teaspoons chili powder
> 1 teaspoon salt
> ½ teaspoon black pepper
> ¼ teaspoon ground red pepper
> 3 pounds beef back ribs, trimmed of excess fat, cut in serving pieces

1. Melt butter in a heavy medium-size saucepan over medium heat. Add onion and garlic; cook 5 minutes, stirring occasionally, until tender.

2. Add ketchup, vinegar, water, sugar, Worcestershire sauce, bay leaf, 1 teaspoon of the mustard, 1 teaspoon of the chili powder, ½ teaspoon of the salt, ¼ teaspoon of the black pepper and ⅛ teaspoon of the ground red pepper to saucepan. Stir well and bring to a boil. Reduce heat to low and simmer 15 to 20 minutes, stirring occasionally, until sauce thickens and flavors have blended. Remove from heat.

3. Prepare barbecue grill or turn on broiler.

4. Mix remaining 1 teaspoon mustard, 1 teaspoon chili powder, ½ teaspoon salt, ¼ teaspoon black pepper and ⅛ teaspoon ground red pepper in a cup. Rub mixture on ribs.

5. To grill: Arrange ribs directly on grill rack about 5 inches above medium-hot coals. Grill about 20 minutes, turning several times, until meat is tender and cooked through.

To broil: Arrange ribs on broiler-pan rack. Broil about 5 inches from heat source about 20 minutes, turning several times, until meat is tender and cooked through.

6. To serve: Arrange ribs on a heated platter. Bring sauce to a boil and pour into a sauceboat to pass on the side.

Makes 4 servings ribs and about 1¼ cups sauce. Per serving ribs with 2 tablespoons sauce: 611 calories, 26 grams protein, 4 grams carbohydrate, 54 grams fat, 135 milligrams cholesterol with butter, 116 milligrams cholesterol with margarine, 684 milligrams sodium

⏱ **MAKE-AHEAD**

Light Dilled Potato Salad

This new version of America's favorite salad won first prize in our *Woman's Day* and Hellmann's—Best Foods Mayonnaise Potato-Salad Contest. This blue-ribbon salad is not only scrumptious, it's easy on the waistline.

> 4 pounds small red or white thin-skinned potatoes, scrubbed
> 2 tablespoons olive oil
> 2 tablespoons cider vinegar
> 1 cup light mayonnaise
> 1 cup plain nonfat yogurt
> 2 tablespoons Dijon mustard
> 1½ teaspoons salt
> ½ teaspoon pepper
> 1 cup minced red onion
> ½ cup minced fresh dill

1. Put potatoes in a large saucepan or Dutch oven and add cold water to cover. Cover saucepan and bring to a boil over high heat. Reduce heat to low and simmer 20 to 30 minutes, until potatoes are tender when pierced with a fork. Drain in a colander and let stand until cool.

2. Cut potatoes in ¾-inch chunks and put in a large bowl. Sprinkle with olive oil and vinegar and toss gently to coat.

3. Mix mayonnaise, yogurt, mustard, salt and pepper in a medium-size bowl. Stir in onion and dill. Pour mixture over potatoes and toss gently to coat well.

4. Cover and chill at least 1 hour and up to 24. Serve chilled.

Makes 9½ cups. Per ½ cup: 120 calories, 3 grams protein, 15 grams carbohydrate, 6 grams fat, 4 milligrams cholesterol, 297 milligrams sodium

Grilled Beef Short Ribs

Beef flanken short ribs are cut crosswise from the sixth, seventh and eighth ribs. Each piece should contain three crosscut rib bones. If you don't see them in the meat case, you can special-order them from your butcher. Ribs and cole slaw are a classic combination.

½ cup medium-sweet sherry wine
    or water
½ cup soy sauce
¼ cup packed brown sugar
¼ cup vegetable oil
2 large cloves garlic, crushed with the
    flat side of a large chef's knife
½ teaspoon pepper
4 pounds beef flanken short ribs,
    about ½-inch thick, trimmed of
    excess fat
1 cup Barbecue Sauce (recipe follows)
For garnish: snipped fresh chives
    (optional)

1. Bring sherry and soy sauce to a boil in a medium-size saucepan over high heat.

2. Stir in sugar. Reduce heat to low. Cover and simmer 5 minutes, until sugar dissolves. Remove from heat. Whisk in oil, garlic and pepper and let cool completely.

3. Place ribs in a large shallow bowl. Pour on marinade and turn ribs to coat. Cover and marinate in refrigerator 3 to 12 hours, turning ribs occasionally.

4. Prepare barbecue grill or turn on broiler.

5. Drain ribs; discard marinade.

6. To grill: Place ribs directly on grill rack 4 to 6 inches above hot coals. Grill 10 minutes for medium-rare, 12 minutes for medium and 14 minutes for well done, turning and basting with Barbecue Sauce twice.

To broil: Place ribs on broiler-pan rack and broil 4 to 6 inches from heat source as directed.

7. Remove ribs to a heated serving platter; pass Barbecue Sauce on the side.

Makes 8 servings. Per serving (with sherry; without additional Barbecue Sauce): 267 calories, 19 grams protein, 8 grams carbohydrate, 16 grams fat, 57 milligrams cholesterol, 481 milligrams sodium

Barbecue Sauce

1½ cups tomato ketchup
1 cup strong black coffee
½ cup packed brown sugar
½ cup Worcestershire sauce
½ cup vegetable oil
⅓ cup cider vinegar

1. Whisk all ingredients in a medium-size saucepan (not uncoated aluminum).

2. Place over medium-high heat and bring to a boil. Reduce heat to low and simmer 5 minutes, whisking occasionally, to blend flavors. Remove from heat.

Makes 4 cups. Per 1 tablespoon: 30 calories, 0 grams protein, 4 grams carbohydrate, 2 grams fat, 0 milligrams cholesterol, 89 milligrams sodium

Note: This sauce will keep up to 3 months in the refrigerator.

Cole Slaw

What are ribs without cole slaw? The flavor of this salad improves on standing, so prepare and refrigerate it at least one day ahead.

1 medium-size head (1¼ pounds)
    green cabbage, coarsely shredded
    (about 7 cups)
¾ cup chopped green bell pepper
¾ cup sliced green onions
¾ cup mayonnaise
2 tablespoons cider vinegar
2 tablespoons granulated sugar
¾ teaspoon celery seed
¾ teaspoon salt
½ teaspoon pepper

1. Mix all ingredients in a medium-size bowl until well blended. Cover and refrigerate for a minimum of 1 but no more than 3 days.

2. To serve: Stir, then transfer cole slaw to a serving dish with a slotted spoon, draining off excess dressing. Serve chilled.

Makes 8 servings. Per serving: 183 calories, 1 gram protein, 9 grams carbohydrate, 17 grams fat, 14 milligrams cholesterol, 339 milligrams sodium

Beef Steaks

Plain and simple, sliced and stir-fried, marinated and grilled, sautéed and sauced, whatever satisfies your taste for steak, you're sure to enjoy a dish made from one of the recipes that follow.

Oriental Flank Steak with Vegetables and Rice

Flank Steak

Flank steaks are long flat steaks about 1-inch thick in the center or thickest portion and generally sold whole, weighing from 1¼ to 2 pounds. Before cooking, trim off any fat from the tips of the steak. It is most tender and flavorful cooked rare to medium-rare.

The grain (or fibers) of flank steak runs lengthwise. It is very easy to see, making this steak a cinch to carve. Holding the knife at an angle to the meat and starting at one short end, cut it crosswise in thin slices.

Oriental Flank Steak with Vegetables and Rice

Complete the meal with this five-minute dessert: Slice peeled bananas into dessert dishes. Stir a carton of strawberry yogurt and spoon it over the bananas.

¼ cup soy sauce
¼ cup water
1 tablespoon cornstarch
1 tablespoon Oriental sesame oil
One 1¼-pound beef flank steak, trimmed of all visible fat
2 tablespoons vegetable oil
2 medium-size red bell peppers, cut in narrow strips
6 ounces snow-peas, trimmed
1½ teaspoons grated fresh gingerroot
1 teaspoon minced fresh garlic
3 cups freshly cooked white rice (1 cup uncooked rice simmered in 2 cups water)
Garnish: 2 chopped green onions plus whole green onions

1. Mix soy sauce, water, cornstarch and sesame oil in a large shallow baking dish. Add steak and turn to coat both sides. Marinate at room temperature 15 minutes.

2. Heat vegetable oil in a large skillet over medium-high heat until hot but not smoking. Lift steak from marinade, letting excess drip off. Reserve marinade. Carefully put steak in skillet (watch out for spatters) and cook 3 to 4 minutes per side, until brown. Steak will be medium-rare. Remove to a cutting board.

3. Add bell-pepper strips, snow-peas, gingerroot and garlic to skillet and stir-fry 1 to 2 minutes, until crisp-tender.

4. Add reserved marinade to skillet and cook 2 minutes, stirring occasionally, until thickened and clear.

5. Slice steak on an angle across the grain in thin slices. Arrange on a heated platter. Spoon rice onto one side of platter. Remove vegetables from skillet with a slotted spoon and arrange on platter. Pour the remaining cooked marinade over meat. Sprinkle chopped green onions over meat and rice; garnish with whole green onions and serve.

Makes 4 servings. Per serving: 501 calories, 36 grams protein, 44 grams carbohydrate, 19 grams fat, 96 milligrams cholesterol, 1,444 milligrams sodium

♥ LOW-CALORIE

Peppered Flank Steak with Onions

Serve with steamed new potatoes tossed with butter and chopped fresh parsley.

One 2-pound beef flank steak, trimmed of all visible fat
1½ tablespoons coarsely ground pepper
Salt to taste
2 tablespoons olive or vegetable oil
2 large onions, sliced (about 4 cups)
2 tablespoons balsamic or cider vinegar
1 teaspoon Worcestershire sauce

1. Remove broiler pan from oven. Turn on broiler.

2. Rub pepper onto both sides of steak. Place on broiler-pan rack and broil 2 to 3 inches from heat source 5 minutes per side for medium-rare, 7 to 8 minutes per side for medium. Transfer steak to a cutting board and season with salt. Let stand 5 minutes.

3. Meanwhile, heat oil in a large nonstick skillet over medium-high heat. Add onions and cook 8 to 10 minutes, stirring occasionally, until golden brown. Add vinegar and Worcestershire sauce and let bubble 1 minute. Remove from heat.

4. Slice steak on an angle across the grain in thin slices. Arrange on a heated platter. Spoon onions over steak and serve.

Makes 8 servings. Per serving: 237 calories, 24 grams protein, 7 grams carbohydrate, 12 grams fat, 57 milligrams cholesterol, 80 milligrams sodium

Stuffed Flank Steak

Skewered and grilled red and yellow cherry tomatoes go well with this delicious rolled steak. A fresh mixed green salad completes the meal.

One 2-pound beef flank steak, trimmed
        of all visible fat
1 braunschweiger liver sausage
        (8 ounces)
8 ounces lean ground pork
8 ounces mushrooms, coarsely
        chopped (about 2½ cups)
1 medium-size green bell pepper,
        diced (about ½ cup)
1 small onion, finely chopped (about
        ¼ cup)
2 teaspoons dried oregano leaves
1 teaspoon minced fresh garlic
1 teaspoon dried basil leaves
½ cup packaged plain dry bread crumbs
Coarsely ground black pepper to taste

1. Put flank steak flat on a waxed-paper-lined baking sheet. Place in freezer 15 minutes to make butterflying easier.

2. To butterfly: Remove steak from freezer. Hold meat flat on work surface with one hand. Starting from thicker end, cut meat horizontally in half to within ½ inch of opposite end.

3. Open meat flat like a book or the wings of a butterfly. Pound with a meat mallet to an even ⅜-inch thickness. Spread liver sausage evenly over surface of meat to within 1 inch of edges.

4. Crumble pork into a large skillet over medium heat. Stir in mushrooms, bell pepper, onion, oregano, garlic and basil and cook 7 to 10 minutes, stirring occasionally, until pork is no longer pink. Remove from heat and pour off juices. Stir in bread crumbs.

5. Prepare barbecue grill or heat oven to 400°F.

6. Place meat on work surface with a long side nearest you. Spread pork mixture lengthwise across flank steak, starting 2 inches in from side nearest you to within 1 inch of the short sides and the side away from you. Fold in the short sides of the steak 1 inch at each end. Then starting from side nearest you, roll up meat tightly like a jelly roll, making a long, thin roast.

7. Tie roast with white string at 1-inch intervals. Rub roast with pepper.

8. To grill: Place roast directly on grill rack 4 to 6 inches above hot coals. Close grill hood or cover roast with a loose foil tent. Grill 22 to 27 minutes, turning roast five times, until a meat thermometer inserted in thickest part of meat, not in the stuffing, registers 135°F.

To roast: Place roast on broiler-pan rack. Roast 22 to 27 minutes, turning five times, until done as directed.

9. Transfer roast to a cutting board. Let stand 15 minutes; internal temperature should rise to 140°F.

10. Remove strings. Cut meat in 1-inch slices. Arrange on a heated platter and serve.

Makes 6 servings. Per serving: 462 calories, 45 grams protein, 10 grams carbohydrate, 26 grams fat, 179 milligrams cholesterol, 630 milligrams sodium

Stuffed Flank Steak

Flank Steak Dinner

Flank Steak Dinner

Use homemade pesto sauce or purchase some at the supermarket. It's usually found in the refrigerator case near the fresh pasta.

2 tablespoons coarsely ground pepper
One 1½-pound beef flank steak,
    trimmed of all visible fat
1 bag (24 ounces) frozen potato wedges
    with skin
2 medium-size fresh ripe tomatoes
4 teaspoons pesto sauce
4 teaspoons packaged Italian-style
    bread crumbs

1. Remove broiler pan from oven. Turn on broiler.

2. Rub pepper onto both sides of steak. Put in middle of broiler-pan rack. Spread out potatoes on one side. Broil steak and potatoes 2 to 3 inches from heat source 4 minutes.

3. Meanwhile, cut tomatoes in half. Spread each cut side with 1 teaspoon of the pesto and sprinkle each with 1 teaspoon of the bread crumbs.

4. Turn steak and potatoes. Arrange tomatoes on empty side of rack and broil 2 minutes.

5. Cover tomatoes lightly with a sheet of foil and broil all 2 minutes longer. Turn steak and potatoes again. Broil 2 minutes longer for medium-rare or until done to taste and potatoes are crisp.

6. Remove steak to a cutting board. Transfer potatoes and tomatoes to a heated platter. Cut steak on an angle across the grain in thin slices. Arrange on the platter and serve.

Makes 4 servings. Per serving: 402 calories, 40 grams protein, 36 grams carbohydrate, 10 grams fat, 116 milligrams cholesterol, 169 milligrams sodium

Steak and Bean Tacjitas

A cross between tacos and fajitas.

8 taco shells
1 tablespoon vegetable oil
1 cup frozen or fresh chopped onion
One 8-ounce beef flank steak, trimmed
    of all visible fat and thinly sliced
    (about 1½ cups) (see Slicing
    Steaks, page 41)
1 tablespoon chili powder
1 can (16 ounces) pinto beans, rinsed
    and drained
1 can (4 ounces) chopped green chiles,
    undrained
3 tablespoons mild, medium or hot
    chunky salsa (from a jar)
2 cups finely shredded iceberg lettuce
½ cup shredded Cheddar cheese
    (2 ounces)
For garnish: hot red peppers (optional)

1. Turn on oven to 250°F. Separate taco shells on a baking sheet. Heat in oven while preparing filling.

2. Heat oil in a large skillet or wok over medium-high heat until hot but not smoking. Add onion and flank-steak slices and stir-fry 4 minutes, until onion starts to brown and meat is no longer pink. Stir in chili powder and stir-fry 30 seconds to release flavors.

3. Add beans, chiles and their liquid, and salsa to skillet and bring to a boil. Reduce heat to low and simmer 5 minutes, stirring once or twice, until mixture is hot and flavors are blended.

4. To assemble tacjitas: Spoon beef mixture into heated taco shells; top with lettuce and cheese.

5. Arrange on dinner plates. Garnish plates with red peppers, if desired, and serve.

Makes 4 servings. Per serving: 414 calories, 25 grams protein, 36 grams carbohydrate, 19 grams fat, 53 milligrams cholesterol, 351 milligrams sodium

Steak and Bean Tacjitas

Flank Steak with Potatoes and Corn

America's favorite, steak and potatoes, in less than 25 minutes—and with just one pot to wash. Good with a mixed green salad.

One 12-ounce beef flank steak, trimmed of all visible fat and thinly sliced (about 2 cups) (see Slicing Steaks, at right)
3 tablespoons Worcestershire sauce
1 teaspoon minced fresh garlic
¼ teaspoon pepper
3 tablespoons plus 1 teaspoon vegetable oil
6 medium-size green onions, cut in 1½-inch pieces
1 cup frozen corn kernels
3 cups frozen O'Brien potatoes (from a 24-ounce bag), thawed
½ teaspoon salt

1. Mix flank-steak slices, Worcestershire sauce, garlic and pepper in a medium-size bowl.

2. Place a Dutch oven over high heat about 3 minutes until very hot. Add 1 tablespoon of the oil and tilt pot to coat bottom. Add beef mixture and stir-fry 1½ to 2 minutes, until no longer pink. Spoon beef and juices into a large bowl.

3. Heat 1 more teaspoon oil in Dutch oven. Add green onions and corn and stir-fry 1 minute, until crisp-tender. Add to beef.

4. Heat remaining 2 tablespoons oil in Dutch oven. Add potatoes and stir-fry 3 minutes, until tender. Add juices from bowl of beef. Stir-fry potatoes 1 minute longer, scraping up browned bits on bottom of Dutch oven.

5. Add meat and vegetables to potatoes. Sprinkle with salt and stir-fry 1 minute.

6. Transfer to a large heated bowl and serve.

Makes 4 servings. Per serving: 333 calories, 22 grams protein, 26 grams carbohydrate, 16 grams fat, 58 milligrams cholesterol, 522 milligrams sodium

Flank Steak with Potatoes and Corn

Beef Strips Pizzaiola

3 tablespoons olive oil
1 large onion, sliced (about 2 cups)
1 large green bell pepper, cut in strips
½ teaspoon minced fresh garlic
One 1¼-pound beef flank steak, trimmed of all visible fat, thinly sliced (see Slicing Steaks, below)
⅓ cup dry red wine
½ teaspoon *each* salt, pepper and dried oregano leaves
1 can (8 ounces) tomato sauce
2 tablespoons drained capers (optional)

1. Heat 2 tablespoons of the oil in a large heavy skillet over high heat. Stir in onion, bell pepper and garlic and cook 5 minutes, stirring frequently, until onion is golden. Remove to a paper towel with slotted spoon.

2. Add remaining tablespoon oil to skillet and heat. Add half the flank-steak sliced and brown, turning often. Remove with slotted spoon to a plate. Repeat with remaining beef. Return first batch of beef to skillet.

3. Add wine and seasonings, stirring to scrape up browned bits on bottom of skillet. Add tomato sauce; bring to a boil. Reduce heat to low. Cover and simmer 15 to 20 minutes, until meat is tender. Add onion mixture and capers, if desired. Cover and cook 2 minutes longer.

4. Transfer to a heated platter and serve.

Makes 4 servings. Per serving: 414 calories, 30 grams protein, 9 grams carbohydrate, 28 grams fat, 96 milligrams cholesterol, 756 milligrams sodium

Slicing Steaks

☐ In many recipes, flank steak or round steak is cut in thin slices before cooking. Unwrap steak and trim off all visible fat. Lay steak flat on a baking sheet lined with waxed paper. Freeze for about 15 minutes or until firm. Remove steak to a cutting board. If steak is wide, halve it lengthwise. Then, with a long sharp knife held at a slight angle to the cutting board, cut meat crosswise across the grain in ½-inch- or ¼-inch-thick slices.

☐ If you don't want to use the steak slices right away, freeze for future use: Arrange slices in a single layer on a waxed-paper-lined baking sheet. If necessary, cover with waxed paper and add a second layer. Freeze 1 to 1½ hours, until hard. Pack airtight, label and store up to 6 months. There's no need to thaw before cooking.

Stir-fried Steak Strips with Peppers and Onions

♥ **LOW-CALORIE**

Stir-fried Steak Strips with Peppers and Onions

Serve with rice or noodles.

2 tablespoons olive oil
One 1-pound beef flank steak, trimmed
    of all visible fat and thinly sliced
    (see Slicing Steaks, page 41)
1 large red bell pepper, cut in 1-inch
    chunks (about 1 cup)
6 medium-size green onions, cut in
    1-inch pieces (about ½ cup)
2½ teaspoons minced fresh garlic
1¼ cups 8-vegetable juice
2 tablespoons Worcestershire sauce
1½ teaspoons dried thyme leaves
Pepper to taste

1. Heat 1 tablespoon of the oil in a large skillet over medium-high heat until hot but not smoking. Add flank-steak slices and stir-fry 1½ to 2 minutes, until lightly browned. (Meat will be rare.) Transfer meat to a plate with a slotted spoon.

2. Add remaining 1 tablespoon oil to skillet. When oil is hot, add bell pepper, green onions and garlic. Stir-fry 2 to 3 minutes, until vegetables are crisp-tender.

3. Stir in vegetable juice, Worcestershire sauce, thyme and pepper. Cook 2 minutes, stirring occasionally, to develop flavor.

4. Return steak slices to skillet and cook 1 minute, stirring constantly, until hot.

5. Transfer to a large heated bowl and serve.

Makes 4 servings. Per serving: 264 calories, 26 grams protein, 9 grams carbohydrate, 13 grams fat, 77 milligrams cholesterol, 344 milligrams sodium

Stir-frying

In this Oriental method, small pieces of food are cooked in a large pot, skillet, wok or Dutch oven over very high heat for a short time in a small amount of oil. To keep food from sticking to the pot: Stir and toss it constantly with one or two long-handled spoons or a spoon and a pancake turner. Have all ingredients assembled and ready to go before you begin because the cooking goes very quickly.

Stir-fried Beef, Peppers and Snow-Peas

The classic accompaniment to a stir-fry is rice, but whole-wheat noodles or spaghetti are equally good with this dish. There's no need to peel fresh gingerroot before grating it.

  1 tablespoon cornstarch
  1 tablespoon soy sauce
  1 tablespoon dry sherry wine or water
  1 teaspoon honey
One 10-ounce beef flank steak, trimmed of all visible fat and thinly sliced (about 2 cups) (see Slicing Steaks, page 41)
  3 tablespoons vegetable oil
  2 large green bell peppers, cut in ¼-inch chunks (about 2 cups)
  8 ounces snow-peas, trimmed (about 2 cups)
 ⅔ cup thinly sliced green onions
  6 ounces fresh mung bean sprouts (about 2¼ loosely packed cups)
1½ teaspoons grated fresh gingerroot
 ½ teaspoon crushed red-pepper flakes

1. Mix cornstarch, soy sauce, sherry and honey in a medium-size bowl. Add flank-steak slices and stir to coat. Marinate 15 minutes at room temperature.

2. Heat oil in a wok or a large deep skillet over medium-high heat until hot but not smoking. Add flank-steak slices and stir-fry 1½ to 2 minutes, until lightly browned. (Meat will be rare.) Transfer meat to a plate with a slotted spoon.

3. Add bell peppers, snow-peas, green onions, bean sprouts, gingerroot and crushed red pepper to wok. Stir-fry 2 to 3 minutes, until vegetables are crisp-tender.

4. Return flank-steak slices to wok and stir-fry 2 minutes, until meat is hot.

5. Transfer to a heated platter and serve.

Makes 4 servings. Per serving (with sherry): 220 calories, 19 grams protein, 16 grams carbohydrate, 15 grams fat, 43 milligrams cholesterol, 374 milligrams sodium

Oriental-Style Beef and Vegetables

Serve in bowls over steamed short-grain rice, with the pan juices spooned on top.

  1 pound fresh spinach, coarse stems removed, rinsed and drained
One 1¼-pound beef flank steak, trimmed of all visible fat and thinly sliced (see Slicing Steaks, page 41)
  6 ounces snow-peas, trimmed, or 1 package (6 ounces) frozen Chinese pea pods
  6 large green onions with 2-inch-long green tops, cut in 2-inch pieces
  4 ounces mushrooms, sliced ¼-inch thick
 ½ cup beef broth
 ¼ cup soy sauce
  1 teaspoon minced fresh garlic
  1 teaspoon ground ginger
  1 teaspoon granulated sugar

1. Put spinach in a deep heavy skillet or Dutch oven. Scatter beef, then vegetables over spinach. Mix beef broth, soy sauce, garlic, ginger and sugar in a small bowl and pour into skillet. Bring to a boil over high heat.

2. Reduce heat to low. Cover and simmer 5 to 6 minutes, stirring occasionally, until spinach is wilted, other vegetables are crisp-tender and meat is no longer pink.

3. Transfer to a large heated bowl and serve.

Makes 4 servings. Per serving: 367 calories, 36 grams protein, 15 grams carbohydrate, 19 grams fat, 99 milligrams cholesterol, 1,617 milligrams sodium

Beef and Bok Choy Stir-fry

Serve over rice, buckwheat noodles or barley.

4 tablespoons thinly sliced
    green onions
2 tablespoons reduced-sodium
    soy sauce
2 tablespoons water
1 tablespoon cornstarch
1 teaspoon Oriental sesame oil
1 teaspoon grated fresh gingerroot or
    ½ teaspoon ground ginger
One 12-ounce beef flank steak, trimmed
    of all visible fat and thinly sliced
    (see Slicing Steaks, page 41)
1 teaspoon sesame seed
1 tablespoon vegetable oil
1 pound bok choy, separated into
    stalks, stalks halved lengthwise,
    then cut crosswise in 1-inch pieces
    (about 4 packed cups)
1 large red or green bell pepper, cut in
    ¼-inch-wide strips
½ cup chicken broth or water

1. Mix 3 tablespoons of the green onions, the soy sauce, water, cornstarch, sesame oil and gingerroot in a medium-size bowl. Add flank-steak slices and toss to coat. Marinate at room temperature 15 minutes.

2. Shake or stir sesame seed in a large deep skillet or wok over medium-high heat about 2 minutes, until lightly toasted. Remove to a paper towel.

3. Heat vegetable oil in skillet over medium-high heat until hot but not smoking. With a slotted spoon, transfer steak slices from marinade to skillet. Reserve marinade. Stir-fry 1½ to 2 minutes until lightly browned. (Meat will be rare.) Remove to a plate with a slotted spoon.

4. Add bok choy and bell pepper to skillet. Stir-fry 2 to 3 minutes, until vegetables are crisp-tender.

5. Stir reserved marinade and chicken broth into skillet. Bring to a boil. Let boil 1 minute.

6. Return flank-steak slices to skillet and stir-fry 1 to 2 minutes, until meat is hot and sauce slightly thickened.

7. Transfer to a large heated bowl. Sprinkle with remaining 1 tablespoon green onions and the toasted sesame seed and serve.

Makes 4 servings. Per serving (with broth): 211 calories, 21 grams protein, 9 grams carbohydrate, 10 grams fat, 60 milligrams cholesterol, 489 milligrams sodium

Microwave Method: Mix 3 tablespoons of the green onions, the soy sauce, water, cornstarch, sesame oil and gingerroot in a medium-size bowl. Add flank-steak slices and marinate at room temperature 15 minutes. To toast sesame seed, put in a 6-ounce microwave-safe custard cup and drizzle with ¼ teaspoon vegetable oil. Microwave uncovered on high 3½ to 4½ minutes, stirring once, until lightly toasted. To cook: Omit oil. Transfer meat from marinade to a 3-quart microwave-safe casserole. Microwave uncovered on high 2½ to 3 minutes, stirring three times, until meat is no longer pink. Remove to a plate with a slotted spoon. Add bok choy and bell pepper to juices in bowl and stir to coat. Cover with a lid or vented plastic wrap. Microwave on high 5 to 6 minutes, stirring once, until vegetables are crisp-tender. Stir in reserved marinade and the broth. Cover and microwave 2 to 3½ minutes, stirring once, until sauce is slightly thickened; stir in beef. Microwave uncovered 1½ to 2 minutes, until beef is hot. Continue as directed.

Perfect Rice

Put rice, liquid (water or broth) and seasonings in a medium-size heavy saucepan. Bring to a boil over high heat. Reduce heat to low; cover and simmer without stirring until rice is tender and liquid is absorbed. Let rice stand covered 5 minutes. Fluff with a fork and serve.

Beef and Bok Choy Stir-fry

Round Steak

Boneless top is the best cut of round steak for the recipes that follow. It is fairly tender, especially when marinated or cut in thin slices and stir-fried, and has excellent flavor. Top round steaks are cut from ¾- to 1-inch thick and weigh about 1½ pounds. To cut steaks in thin slices easily, follow the directions on page 41.

🕐 MAKE-AHEAD
London Broil

½ cup vegetable oil
¼ cup lemon juice
¼ cup water
2 tablespoons chopped fresh parsley
1 tablespoon grated onion
1 teaspoon dried marjoram leaves
1 teaspoon dried thyme leaves
1 teaspoon salt
1 teaspoon minced fresh garlic
½ teaspoon hot-pepper sauce
One 2-pound boneless beef top round
    steak, trimmed of all visible fat

1. Mix oil, lemon juice, water, parsley, onion, herbs, salt, garlic and hot-pepper sauce in a shallow baking dish. Add beef and turn to coat. Cover and marinate in refrigerator overnight, turning meat several times.

2. Prepare barbecue grill or turn on broiler.

3. Drain meat; reserve marinade.

4. To grill: Place steak directly on grill rack about 5 inches above medium coals. Grill about 10 minutes per side, basting once with reserved marinade, until rare. (Grill longer if you want steak more well done.)

To broil: Place steak on broiler-pan rack 4 to 5 inches from heat source. Broil about 10 minutes per side, basting once with reserved marinade, until rare.

5. Remove steak to a cutting board and let stand 5 minutes.

6. Cut meat on an angle across the grain in thin slices and arrange on a heated platter. Serve.

Makes 8 servings. Per serving: 448 calories, 23 grams protein, 1 gram carbohydrate, 39 grams fat, 74 milligrams cholesterol, 322 milligrams sodium

---

Basics About Browners

☐ Browning dishes are specially designed and treated with a metal coating so the bottom absorbs microwave energy and gets hot enough to sear and brown the food surface.

☐ Preheat the browner on high; the length of time depends on what you're cooking. Caution: As a browner absorbs microwaves it gets very hot. Handle with pot holders and set browner down only on a heatproof surface. Never touch the bottom; it can burn a pot holder and melt plastic.

☐ Foods are cooked uncovered, so expect some spattering. Transfer food to a serving dish as soon as it's done. Don't damage a browner's coating by cutting on it.

✳ MICROWAVE
Speedy London Broil

Serve with Vegetables with Mustard Vinaigrette (recipe follows).

One 2-pound boneless beef top round
    steak, 1¾- to 2-inches thick,
    trimmed of all visible fat
1½ teaspoons olive oil
1 tablespoon minced fresh garlic
¼ teaspoon salt
⅛ teaspoon pepper

1. Preheat browning dish according to manufacturer's instructions, 6 to 8 minutes depending on brand and size.

2. Meanwhile, rub steak with oil and garlic and season with salt and pepper.

3. Remove hot browner from oven and add steak. In about 2 minutes, when the sizzling stops, turn steak over.

4. Microwave uncovered on high 8 to 10 minutes for medium-rare. (Microwave longer if you want steak more well done.) Immediately transfer meat to cutting board. Let stand 10 minutes.

5. Cut steak on an angle across the grain in thin slices. Arrange on heated platter and serve.

Makes 6 servings. Per serving: 183 calories, 28 grams protein, 1 gram carbohydrate 7 grams fat, 81 milligrams cholesterol, 158 milligrams sodium

Speedy London Broil; Vegetables with Mustard Vinaigrette

✳ MICROWAVE
Vegetables with Mustard Vinaigrette

Microwave assorted vegetables in separate pint-size zipper-closing plastic food bags at one time. Use only bags that are microwave-safe.

Vegetables
1 cup 1½-inch broccoli florets
1 cup 1½-inch cauliflower florets
1 cup ¼-inch-thick slices carrots
1 cup ¼-inch-thick slices yellow summer squash or zucchini
1 cup 2-inch pieces trimmed green beans
1 cup trimmed snow-peas (about 4 ounces)

Mustard Vinaigrette
2 tablespoons red-wine vinegar
2 tablespoons Dijon mustard
½ teaspoon minced fresh garlic
½ teaspoon granulated sugar
½ teaspoon salt
½ cup olive oil

1. Place each vegetable in a pint-size microwave-safe zipper-closing bag. Partially close bags, leaving a 1-inch opening for steam to escape. Arrange on oven floor in a circle, not touching.

2. Microwave on high, rearranging bags once during cooking. Remove each bag as vegetable is done: snow-peas, 5 minutes; broccoli and summer squash, 7 minutes; cauliflower and green beans, 9 minutes; carrots, 10 minutes. Immediately run bags briefly under cold water to stop the cooking; vegetables should still be warm. Drain off any cooking liquid through opening in top.

3. Open bags and arrange vegetables on a heated serving platter.

4. Meanwhile, whisk all dressing ingredients except oil in a small bowl. When well blended, whisk in oil. Pour over warm vegetables and serve.

Makes 6 servings. Per serving: 206 calories, 3 grams protein, 9 grams carbohydrate, 19 grams fat, 0 milligrams cholesterol, 261 milligrams sodium

Blackened Steaks with Vegetables

Inspired by the fiery Cajun-style cooking of chef Paul Prudhomme. Keep the kitchen fan on while making these steaks.

2 teaspoons paprika
1 teaspoon dried Italian-herb
    seasoning
1 teaspoon garlic powder
1 teaspoon onion salt
1 teaspoon ground red pepper
Four 4-ounce boneless beef eye round
    steaks, ½-inch thick, or other
    small frying steaks such as top
    sirloin or chuck steaks
3 tablespoons vegetable oil
3 cups frozen O'Brien potatoes (from a
    24-ounce bag)
½ teaspoon salt
1 pint basket cherry tomatoes (about
    2 cups)
For garnish: fresh parsley sprigs

1. Mix paprika, Italian seasoning, garlic powder, onion salt and ground red pepper on a sheet of waxed paper. Press both sides of steaks into seasonings.

2. Heat a large heavy skillet, preferably cast-iron (not nonstick), over medium-high heat about 2 minutes, until a drop of water flicked onto the surface evaporates almost immediately.

3. Place steaks in hot skillet and cook 2 minutes per side for rare, or until done to taste. Remove to a heated platter; some seasonings will stick to pan. Cover loosely with a sheet of foil to keep warm.

4. Add 2 tablespoons of the oil to skillet; tilt to coat bottom. Add potatoes; sprinkle with salt and cook 8 to 9 minutes, stirring two or three times, until heated through.

5. Meanwhile, heat remaining 1 tablespoon oil in a medium-size skillet over medium-high heat. Add tomatoes and cook, shaking skillet occasionally, until skins start to split.

6. Slice steaks or transfer whole to dinner plates and pour meat juices from platter over them. Serve with potatoes and tomatoes and garnish with parsley sprigs.

Makes 4 servings. Per serving: 439 calories, 26 grams protein, 25 grams carbohydrate, 24 grams fat, 77 milligrams cholesterol, 677 milligrams sodium

Blackened Steaks with Vegetables

Barbecued Beef, Green Pepper and Corn on Buns

Barbecued Beef, Green Pepper and Corn on Buns

For a change, spoon the beef mixture into warm pita pockets or serve it over corn bread.

2 **tablespoons vegetable oil**
One **1-pound boneless beef top round or flank steak, trimmed of all visible fat and thinly sliced (see Slicing Steaks, page 41)**
1 **large green bell pepper, cut in chunks**
2 **green onions, cut in ½-inch pieces**
1 **box (10 ounces) frozen corn kernels**
1 **cup bottled barbecue sauce**
1 **large fresh tomato, cut in chunks**
4 **split and toasted hamburger buns**

1. Heat oil in a large heavy skillet over medium-high heat until hot but not smoking. Add steak slices and stir-fry about 3 minutes, until browned. Remove to a bowl with a slotted spoon.

2. Reduce heat to medium. Add bell pepper and onions to skillet. Cook 5 minutes, stirring occasionally, until tender.

3. Stir in corn, barbecue sauce, tomato and the browned steak slices. Cook 2 to 3 minutes, stirring frequently, until heated through. Remove from heat.

4. Place a hamburger-bun bottom on each of four dinner plates. Top each with one quarter of the beef mixture. Add bun tops and serve.

Makes 4 servings. Per serving: 526 calories, 29 grams protein, 47 grams carbohydrate, 25 grams fat, 61 milligrams cholesterol, 799 milligrams sodium

Oriental Beef and Cabbage

2. Add cabbage, bell pepper and green onions to skillet; stir-fry about 2 minutes, until crisp-tender. Remove to same platter. Add water, sauce mix and sesame oil to skillet. Stir well and cook about 2 minutes, until sauce boils and is smooth and thickened.

3. Return beef and vegetable mixture to skillet. Toss with sauce to coat evenly and heat through. Serve from skillet or spoon into a large heated bowl.

Makes 4 servings. Per serving: 352 calories, 25 grams protein, 11 grams carbohydrate, 23 grams fat, 77 milligrams cholesterol, 507 milligrams sodium

Note: Hunter-sauce mix can be found in the sauce, soup or gourmet section of your market.

Beef with Broccoli

Serve over steamed white or brown rice or chow-mein or lo-mein noodles.

> ½ cup water
> ¼ cup soy sauce
> 2 tablespoons cider vinegar
> 1 beef bouillon cube, crushed
> 1 tablespoon cornstarch
> 4 tablespoons vegetable oil
> 2 large cloves garlic, halved
> One 12-ounce boneless beef top round steak, trimmed of all visible fat and thinly sliced (see Slicing Steaks, page 41)
> 1 large onion, halved and sliced ¼-inch thick
> 3½ cups broccoli florets
> 2 cups sliced mushrooms

1. Mix water, soy sauce, vinegar, bouillon cube and cornstarch in a cup.

2. Heat 2 tablespoons of the oil in a large deep skillet or wok over high heat until hot but not smoking. Add garlic and cook a few seconds, stirring constantly. Add steak slices and stir-fry 2 minutes, until lightly browned but still pink in center. Pour meat and juices into a bowl. Discard garlic.

3. Heat remaining 2 tablespoons oil in skillet. Add onion and stir-fry 2 minutes. Add broccoli and mushrooms and stir-fry 3 minutes.

4. Return steak slices and juices to skillet. Stir soy-sauce mixture again and pour into skillet. Cover and simmer 2 minutes.

5. Uncover skillet and simmer 1 minute, until sauce is thickened. Transfer to a large heated bowl and serve.

Makes 4 servings. Per serving: 371 calories, 24 grams protein, 15 grams carbohydrate, 25 grams fat, 59 milligrams cholesterol, 1,650 milligrams sodium

Oriental Beef and Cabbage

Serve with fried rice.

> 2 tablespoons vegetable oil
> One 1-pound boneless beef top round steak, trimmed of all visible fat and thinly sliced (see Slicing Steaks, page 41)
> 8 ounces green cabbage, coarsely shredded (about 3 packed cups)
> 1 medium-size red bell pepper, cut in ½-inch strips
> 4 green onions, cut in 1-inch lengths
> 1 cup water
> 1 package (1⅛ ounces) hunter-sauce mix (see Note)
> 1 teaspoon Oriental sesame oil

1. Heat vegetable oil in a large skillet or wok over medium-high heat until hot but not smoking. Add steak slices and stir-fry about 4 minutes, until no longer pink. Remove to a serving platter with a slotted spoon.

Stir-fried Steak with Vegetables and Hash Browns

Stir-fried Steak with Vegetables and Hash Browns

2 tablespoons butter or margarine
3 cups (12 ounces) frozen Southern-style hash-brown potatoes
One 1¼-pound boneless beef top round or flank steak, trimmed of all visible fat and thinly sliced (see Slicing Steaks, page 41)
¼ cup dry sherry wine (optional)
⅛ teaspoon minced fresh garlic
1 cup boiling water
¼ teaspoon ground ginger
⅛ teaspoon salt
1 package (1⅛ ounces) Swiss pepper-sauce mix with green peppercorns
1 jar (4 ounces) sliced pimientos, undrained
1 package (14 ounces) frozen Japanese-style stir-fry vegetables

1. Melt butter in a large skillet over high heat. Add potatoes and cook 3 minutes, stirring occasionally, until lightly browned.

2. Add steak slices to skillet and stir-fry 4 minutes, until meat is no longer pink.

3. Add remaining ingredients in order given and stir to mix. Cook 5 minutes, until sauce has thickened and stir-fry vegetables are hot. Remove from heat.

4. Transfer to a large heated bowl and serve.

Makes 4 servings. Per serving: 470 calories, 33 grams protein, 31 grams carbohydrate, 24 grams fat, 114 milligrams cholesterol with butter, 96 milligrams cholesterol with margarine, 863 milligrams sodium

Sirloin Steak

Sirloin steaks, tender and tasty, may be purchased bone-in or boneless. The best buy is a boneless loin top sirloin steak, which contains a piece of the tenderloin. Most markets sell steaks with fat trimmed to less than ¼-inch around the edges, but the trend today is to trim it even more, to ⅛-inch.

★ SPECIAL—AND WORTH IT
Conchas Steaks

Double this recipe to serve eight, or triple it to serve twelve. Fresh corn on the cob and tomatoes and cucumbers tossed with vinaigrette complete the meal. To keep steaks from curling during cooking, slash fat around the edges in three or four places. Use tongs instead of a fork to turn meat; forks pierce the meat, allowing the flavorful juices to run out.

**Four 12-ounce boneless beef sirloin
      steaks, 1-inch thick, or four 1¼-
      pound T-bone steaks, trimmed of
      excess fat**
**4 fresh or drained canned whole green
      chiles, cut in thin strips**
**Four ⅛-inch-thick slices sharp Cheddar
      cheese (about 2 ounces each)**

1. Prepare barbecue grill or turn on broiler.

2. To grill: Arrange steaks directly on grill rack 4 to 6 inches above hot coals. Grill 4 to 6 minutes for rare, 6 to 10 minutes for medium. Turn steaks with tongs. Top with chiles, then cheese. Close grill hood or cover steaks with a foil tent. Grill 4 to 6 minutes longer, until cheese melts and meat is done as desired.

To broil: Arrange steaks on lightly oiled broiler-pan rack. Broil 4 to 6 inches from heat source 4 to 6 minutes. Turn with tongs. Broil second side 4 to 6 minutes. Two minutes before steaks are done, top with chiles and cheese. Turn oven selector to bake and temperature control to 450°F. Continue to cook until cheese is melted and meat is done as desired.

3. Transfer to dinner plates and serve.

Makes 4 servings. Per serving (T-bone): 594 calories, 64 grams protein, 1 gram carbohydrate, 35 grams fat, 206 milligrams cholesterol, 520 milligrams sodium

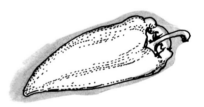

Conchas Steaks

Pepper Steaks

Serve this colorful dish with buttered broccoli spears and rice or crusty bread.

Four 6-ounce boneless beef top loin steaks (club or strip steaks), each about ¾ inches thick, trimmed of excess fat, or four 4-ounce filet mignon steaks, each about 1-inch thick, trimmed of all visible fat
4 teaspoons coarsely cracked black pepper, or to taste
1 teaspoon butter or margarine
⅔ cup diced green bell pepper
⅔ cup diced red bell pepper
1 medium-size onion, sliced in rings
1 teaspoon minced fresh garlic
1 teaspoon vegetable oil
¾ cup bottled mango chutney

1. Sprinkle each side of steaks with ½ teaspoon of the pepper, pressing it in firmly.

2. Melt butter in a large heavy skillet over medium heat. Add bell peppers, onion and garlic. Cook 5 minutes, stirring occasionally, until vegetables are tender. Remove vegetables to a plate with a slotted spoon.

3. Increase heat under skillet to high. Add oil to skillet and heat until hot but not smoking. Add steaks and cook 2 minutes per side for rare. (Cook longer if you want steaks more well done.) Remove to a heated platter.

4. Reduce heat under skillet to low. Add chutney and the bell-pepper mixture to skillet. Cook 1 minute, until hot. Spoon over steaks and serve.

Makes 4 servings. Per serving: 678 calories, 23 grams protein, 33 grams carbohydrate, 50 grams fat, 99 milligrams cholesterol with butter, 87 milligrams cholesterol with margarine, 187 milligrams sodium

Pepper Steaks

Skirt Steak

Skirt steak is a long flat piece of meat, the diaphragm of the animal, weighing from ½ to 1 pound. It has a thin fat covering, which must be trimmed before cooking. Part of the fat will pull off easily if you grasp it with a paper towel, but the remainder must be trimmed with a sharp knife.

The grain runs crosswise and is easy to see. Our recipes call for cutting steaks crosswise in pieces before cooking. To carve a cooked skirt steak, hold the knife at an angle to the meat and thinly cut it crosswise across the grain.

If you can't find skirt steak in your market, use flank steak instead.

⏱ MAKE-AHEAD
Fajitas

A Tex-Mex favorite. If you can't find 12-inch flour tortillas in your market, substitute smaller tortillas and use two for each serving.

1½ pounds beef skirt steaks, trimmed
    of all visible fat, cut crosswise in
    6 pieces
Juice of 3 small limes (about ¼ cup)
  1 tablespoon minced fresh garlic
  ½ teaspoon kosher (coarse) salt
  ½ teaspoon crushed red-pepper flakes
    or ground black pepper, or to
    taste
Six 12-inch flour tortillas
  1 tablespoon vegetable oil
12 leaves romaine or curly leaf lettuce,
    rinsed and dried
Guacamole (recipe follows)
  1 medium-size fresh tomato,
    chopped (about ½ cup)
  1 medium-size onion, chopped
    (about ½ cup)
  ¼ cup coarsely chopped fresh cilantro
Sour cream or plain yogurt and
    prepared salsa

1. Flatten steak pieces to a ¼-inch thickness with a meat mallet or the bottom of a heavy skillet.

2. Put lime juice in a pie plate. Add 1 piece of steak; press into juice, sprinkle with minced garlic and some of the salt and pepper. Push to one side of pie plate. Repeat with remaining pieces, stacking them as they're seasoned. Cover and marinate 30 minutes at room temperature, turning steaks twice.

3. Heat oven to 250°F. Stack tortillas and wrap in foil. Warm in oven along with six ovenproof dinner plates about 15 minutes.

4. Meanwhile, heat oil in a large heavy skillet over high heat until hot but not smoking. Add steaks and cook 2 to 2½ minutes per side for medium-rare.

5. Remove steaks to a cutting board and thinly slice on an angle across the grain.

6. To assemble: Put a warm tortilla on each plate and arrange 2 lettuce leaves side by side in the center. Top with sliced steak, Guacamole, tomato, onion, cilantro, sour cream and salsa. Fold ends of tortilla over part of filling, then fold in sides. Serve remaining Guacamole and additional sour cream and salsa on the side.

Makes 6 servings. Per serving with 1 tablespoon each Guacamole and sour cream: 333 calories, 20 grams protein, 39 grams carbohydrate, 19 grams fat, 47 milligrams cholesterol, 262 milligrams sodium

Guacamole

  2 ripe avocados (about 9 ounces
    each), halved, pitted, peeled and
    cut in ½-inch chunks
  1 small fresh tomato, finely chopped
    (about ⅓ cup)
  2 tablespoons thinly sliced
    green onion
  1 tablespoon chopped fresh cilantro
  1 teaspoon minced fresh garlic
  ¾ teaspoon salt
  2 tablespoons drained canned
    chopped hot green chiles, or to
    taste
1½ teaspoons fresh-squeezed lime
    juice, or to taste

1. Mix all ingredients except the chiles and lime juice in a medium-size bowl. Add chiles and lime juice, stirring gently to blend.

2. Cover and refrigerate up to 1 hour.

Makes 2 cups. Per ¼ cup: 67 calories, 1 gram protein, 3 grams carbohydrate, 6 grams fat, 0 milligrams cholesterol, 201 milligrams sodium

Fajitas

Parrilla Venezolana with Salsa Guasacaca

A traditional Latin-American barbecue specialty. Serve with Arepas (recipe follows), which are small disks made of hominy (dried kernels of skinned white corn), seasoned and fried until crisp. Arepas provide a perfect foil to the spicy meat and salsa.

```
3  cups orange juice
½  cup chopped onion
2  tablespoons dried oregano leaves
2  tablespoons coarse ground pepper
1  tablespoon minced fresh garlic
1  teaspoon meat tenderizer
1  teaspoon salt
2½ pounds beef skirt steaks, trimmed
   of all visible fat, cut crosswise in
   4 to 6 pieces
Salsa Guasacaca (recipe follows)
```

1. Mix orange juice, onion, oregano, pepper, garlic, meat tenderizer and salt in a large bowl. Add skirt-steak pieces. Cover and marinate in refrigerator at least 6 hours or overnight.

2. Prepare barbecue grill or turn on broiler.

3. Drain steaks; discard marinade.

4. To grill: Place skirt steaks directly on grill rack 4 to 6 inches above hot coals. Grill 5 minutes per side for medium-rare. (Grill longer if you want steaks more well done.)

To broil: Arrange steaks on broiler-pan rack. Broil 4 to 5 inches from heat source as directed.

5. Transfer steaks to a cutting board and let stand 5 minutes. Cut on an angle across the grain in thin slices and arrange on a heated platter. Serve with Salsa Guasacaca.

Makes 6 servings. Per 4-ounce serving: 320 calories, 41 grams protein, 13 grams carbohydrate, 10 grams fat, 120 milligrams cholesterol, 377 milligrams sodium

Salsa Guasacaca

```
3  ripe avocados (about 8 ounces each),
   halved, pitted, peeled and cut in
   ½-inch cubes
2  medium-size fresh tomatoes,
   chopped (about 1½ cups)
1  large onion, finely chopped (about
   1 cup)
1  large green bell pepper, chopped
   (about 1 cup)
¼  cup white-wine vinegar
¼  cup olive oil
3  tablespoons chopped fresh or
   canned jalapeño peppers (see Note)
1  teaspoon salt
½  teaspoon pepper
```

1. Put all ingredients in a medium-size bowl. Stir gently to mix.

2. Cover and refrigerate up to 2 hours before serving.

Makes 5½ cups. Per ¼ cup: 63 calories, 1 gram protein, 3 grams carbohydrate, 6 grams fat, 0 milligrams cholesterol, 100 milligrams sodium

Note: Remove all or some of the seeds from jalapeños if you prefer less bite to your sauce. Wear rubber gloves and never touch your eyes when working with hot peppers.

Arepas

```
2  cans (16 ounces each) white hominy,
   rinsed and drained
½  teaspoon salt
¼  teaspoon ground red pepper
¼  teaspoon onion powder
2  tablespoons vegetable oil
```

1. Process hominy in food processor (in two batches if necessary) to a smooth paste.

2. Transfer hominy to a medium-size bowl. Stir in salt, ground red pepper and onion powder. Form into eighteen 2-inch patties, about ½-inch thick, using about 2 tablespoons of the mixture for each.

3. Heat oil in a large skillet over medium-high heat. Add arepas in a single layer; cook 3 to 5 minutes per side, until lightly golden. Transfer to a heated platter and serve.

Makes 6 servings. Per serving: 117 calories, 2 grams protein, 17 grams carbohydrate, 5 grams fat, 0 milligrams cholesterol, 178 milligrams sodium

Steak with Beans in Peppers

In this broiler meal, everything's cooked in one pan, making cleanup a breeze. If the vegetables start to burn, cover them with a sheet of foil.

2 medium-size red or green bell
    peppers, halved lengthwise, seeded
    and cored
1 can (16 ounces) small white beans
    such as navy or cannellini, drained
½ cup shredded Monterey Jack cheese
    (2 ounces)
¼ cup sliced green onions
2 tablespoons olive oil
½ teaspoon dried basil leaves
⅛ teaspoon pepper
1 package (9 ounces) frozen French-
    fried onion rings
1 pound beef skirt steak, trimmed of
    all visible fat, cut crosswise in 4
    pieces
⅓ cup bottled barbecue sauce

1. Remove broiler pan from oven. Turn on broiler. Line broiler-pan rack with foil; spray foil with no-stick vegetable cooking spray.

2. Place bell peppers cut-side down on one side of foil-lined rack. Broil 2 to 3 inches from heat source 4 minutes, until skins start to blister and blacken. Turn and broil 1 minute longer.

3. Meanwhile, mix beans, cheese, green onions, oil, basil and pepper in a medium-size bowl. Spoon mixture into bell peppers.

4. Spread onion rings in center of broiler-pan rack. Arrange steaks on the empty side. Brush steaks with half the barbecue sauce.

5. Broil 3 to 4 inches from heat source 3 minutes. Turn steaks and onion rings and brush steaks with remaining sauce. Broil 3 to 5 minutes longer, until meat is done to taste.

6. Transfer steaks and peppers to dinner plates. Top steaks with onions and serve.

Makes 4 servings. Per serving: 1,007 calories, 35 grams protein, 42 grams carbohydrate, 79 grams fat, 100 milligrams cholesterol, 668 milligrams sodium

Steaks with Beans in Peppers

Chuck Steak

The recipes that follow are a good way to cook a lean and relatively inexpensive cut of meat, boneless beef chuck shoulder steak, also called English steak or simply shoulder steak. For best flavor, marinate this cut; for tenderness, cook only to rare or medium-rare. To carve: Hold the knife at a slight angle to the cutting board, and cut steak crosswise across the grain in very thin slices.

🕐 MAKE-AHEAD
Grilled Beef in Beer

The secrets to this recipe are beer and time; the simple marinade adds flavor. Serve with grilled vegetables and your favorite pasta salad.

1 can (12 ounces) beer
½ cup soy sauce
½ cup vegetable oil
⅛ teaspoon pepper
One 2½-pound boneless beef chuck
    shoulder steak, about 1½-inches
    thick, trimmed of excess fat

1. Mix beer, soy sauce, oil and pepper in a shallow dish just large enough to hold the steak. Add steak and turn to coat both sides.

2. Cover and refrigerate 8 to 24 hours, turning three or four times.

3. Prepare barbecue grill or turn on broiler.

4. Drain steak; discard marinade.

5. To grill: Place steak directly on grill rack 4 to 6 inches above medium-hot coals. Grill 5 minutes per side for rare, 7 minutes per side for medium-rare. (Grill longer if you want steak more well done.)

To broil: Place steak on broiler-pan rack. Broil 4 to 6 inches from heat source 5 minutes per side for rare, 7 minutes per side for medium-rare.

6. Remove steak to a cutting board. Cover loosely with a sheet of foil to keep warm. Let stand 10 minutes.

7. Cut steak on an angle across the grain in ¼-inch-thick slices. Arrange on a heated platter and serve.

Makes 8 servings. Per serving: 316 calories, 27 grams protein, 2 grams carbohydrate, 20 grams fat, 89 milligrams cholesterol, 713 milligrams sodium

🕐 MAKE-AHEAD
♥ LOW-CALORIE
Grilled Chuck Steak

Great for a cookout. Cole slaw or potato salad and wedges of chilled watermelon complete the meal.

One 2-pound boneless beef chuck
    shoulder steak, 1½-inches thick,
    trimmed of all visible fat
½ cup bottled Italian dressing
¼ cup sliced green onions

1. Place chuck steak in a large shallow pan. Add dressing and turn to coat. Cover and marinate in refrigerator at least 1 hour.

2. Prepare barbecue grill or turn on broiler.

3. Drain steak; discard marinade.

4. To grill: Place steak directly on grill rack 4 to 6 inches above hot coals. Grill 5 minutes per side for rare, 7 minutes per side for medium-rare. (Grill longer if you want steak more well done.)

To broil: Place steak on broiler-pan rack. Broil 4 to 6 inches from heat source 5 minutes per side for rare, 7 minutes per side for medium-rare.

5. Remove steak to a cutting board and cover loosely with a sheet of foil to keep warm. Let stand 10 minutes.

6. Cut steak on an angle across the grain in ¼-inch-thick slices. Arrange on a heated platter; sprinkle with green onion; serve immediately.

Makes 6 to 8 servings. Per 3-ounce serving: 205 calories, 23 grams protein, 0 grams carbohydrate, 12 grams fat, 62 milligrams cholesterol, 104 milligrams sodium

Grilled Beef in Beer

Ground Beef

*We've collected our favorite ground beef recipes—
and not just for burgers, though they're here—
but also for mouth-watering meatloaf, taste-tempting casseroles,
flavorful meatballs and delicious chili.*

The J.T. Burger

Ground Beef

☐ **What It Is:** Ground beef is, by definition, boned meat without added fat, seasoning, water, binders or extenders. If prepared in a federally- or state-inspected plant according to USDA regulations, the finished product contains no more than 30 percent fat. Ground beef is sold labeled by either the cut or the percentage of lean to fat, depending on your supermarket's meat-labeling policy.

85% lean; may also be called ground round or sirloin
80% lean; may also be called ground chuck
70% lean; may also be called ground beef

☐ **Keep It Lean:** Our recipes call for lean ground beef, which refers to 85% lean (ground round or sirloin), however, you may use 80% lean (ground chuck) with equal success. To remove as much fat as possible, pour off and discard drippings after browning meat or blot browned meat with paper towels. Skim fat from the top of chilis.

☐ **Handle with Care:** Handle lean ground beef gently. Don't pack or compress it too much. If adding ingredients to the beef for burgers, meatballs or meat loaves, mix it with your hands, using a light touch, or with two forks, which will fluff the meat instead of compressing it. Some markets now carry 90% lean ground beef, but this requires very carefully handling and cooking because the lack of fat tends to make it dry; fat adds flavor and juiciness to meat.

Cook ground beef within two days of purchasing, or wrap it well and freeze up to four months.

Fresh Herbs

☐ Many supermarkets now stock a variety of fresh herbs. As a general rule, replace one tablespoon fresh herbs with one teaspoon dried.

☐ The finer herbs are minced, the more flavorful they are. Mince them with scissors for speed, or chop them with a chef's knife.

☐ Don't wash herbs until you're ready to use them. Most herbs will keep up to one week in the refrigerator with the stems standing in water in a jar. Cover leaves loosely with a plastic bag. Change the water every two days. To use: Wash the herbs and strip leaves from the stems; discard stems.

Hamburgers

★ **SPECIAL—AND WORTH IT**
The J.T. Burger

This burger was developed for *Woman's Day* by the famous California chef Jeremiah Tower—it's a garlic lover's dream.

6 **very large cloves garlic, peeled**
About ¾ **cup chicken broth**
1 **pound lean ground beef**
2 **large crusty buns, preferably sourdough, split and toasted**
Mint Aioli (recipe follows)

1. Put garlic in a small saucepan and add just enough chicken broth to cover. Bring to a boil over high heat. Reduce heat to low. Cover and simmer 10 minutes, until garlic is soft. Drain garlic; let cool slightly and slice thin.

2. Prepare barbecue grill or turn on broiler.

3. Shape beef into 2 patties. Arrange patties directly on grill rack about 4 inches above hot coals. Grill 4 minutes per side for rare. (Grill longer if you want burgers more well done.)

To broil: Arrange patties on broiler-pan rack. Broil 4 to 6 inches from heat source 4 minutes per side for rare.

4. Spread each toasted bun with 1 tablespoon Mint Aioli and top with cooked burgers. Arrange sliced garlic on top, close buns and serve.

Makes 2 servings. Per serving with 1 tablespoon sauce: 742 calories, 46 grams protein, 39 grams carbohydrate, 43 grams fat, 150 milligrams cholesterol, 594 milligrams sodium

Mint Aioli
⅓ **cup mayonnaise**
1 **tablespoon finely chopped fresh mint leaves**
1 **teaspoon fresh-squeezed lemon juice**
½ **teaspoon finely minced fresh garlic**
Pinch of pepper

1. Mix all ingredients in a small bowl. Cover and chill up to 1 week. Serve with J.T. Burgers.

Makes ⅓ cup. Per tablespoon: 105 calories, 0 grams protein, 1 gram carbohydrate, 12 grams fat, 9 milligrams cholesterol, 83 milligrams sodium

Mozzarella-Stuffed Burgers

Serve these burgers on good rolls with slices of ripe tomatoes and red onion. Shoestring potatoes will add a nice crunch.

1½ **pounds lean ground beef**
 ½ **cup packaged seasoned dry bread crumbs**
 1 **large egg**
 1 **tablespoon dried Italian-herb seasoning**
 ¼ **teaspoon salt**
 ¼ **teaspoon pepper**
 4 **ounces mozzarella cheese, cut in ½-inch cubes (about ¾ cup)**

1. Mix beef, bread crumbs, egg and seasonings in a medium-size bowl with hands or two forks until blended. Shape mixture into twelve 3-inch patties.

2. Top 6 of the patties with the cheese cubes, piling them up in the center. Cover each with another patty; press edges to seal.

3. Prepare barbecue grill or turn on broiler.

4. To grill: Arrange patties directly on grill rack 4 to 6 inches above hot coals. Grill 4 minutes per side for rare, 5 minutes per side for medium.

To broil: Place burgers on broiler-pan rack. Broil 4 to 5 inches from heat source as directed.

5. Transfer burgers to dinner plates or sandwich in buns and serve.

Makes 6 servings. Per serving: 333 calories, 26 grams protein, 7 grams carbohydrate, 22 grams fat, 134 milligrams cholesterol, 279 milligrams sodium

Sun-Dried Tomato, Smoked Mozzarella and Basil Burgers

Look for tomatoes dried without salt; they will have a more intense, sweet-tomato flavor. We liked these burgers without buns, but you could add a bun or serve on thick slices of toasted French bread.

1½ **pounds lean ground beef**
Pepper to taste
 4 **slices (1 ounce each) smoked mozzarella cheese**
 8 **oil-cured sun-dried tomatoes**
 8 **fresh basil leaves**

1. Prepare barbecue grill or turn on broiler.

2. Shape beef into four 1-inch-thick patties. Season with pepper.

3. To grill: Place patties directly on grill rack 4 to 6 inches above hot coals. Grill 3 minutes. Turn and grill 5 minutes longer for rare, 8 minutes for medium, 12 minutes for well-done. Two minutes before burgers are done, top with cheese. Grill until cheese starts to melt.

To broil: Broil 4 to 6 inches from heat source 6 minutes per side for rare, 8 minutes per side for medium, 10 minutes for well-done. Top burgers with cheese and broil 1 minute longer, until cheese starts to melt.

4. Transfer burgers to plates, top with sun-dried tomatoes and basil and serve.

Makes 4 servings. Per serving (with tomatoes dried without salt): 691 calories, 37 grams protein, 11 grams carbohydrate, 56 grams fat, 127 milligrams cholesterol, 440 milligrams sodium

♥ **LOW-CALORIE**
Basil Burgers

Serve these with lightly toasted sesame buns and a crisp lettuce and radish salad on the side.

1⅓ **pounds lean ground beef**
 1 **cup finely chopped sweet red onion**
 1 **cup finely chopped fresh basil leaves or 2 teaspoons crumbled dried basil**
 1 **teaspoon salt**
 ½ **teaspoon pepper, or to taste**
 4 **large thick slices tomato**
For garnish: fresh basil sprigs (optional)

1. Mix beef, onion, basil, salt and pepper in a large bowl with hands or two forks until well blended. Shape into four 1-inch-thick patties.

2. Cook patties in a large heavy skillet over medium heat about 5 minutes per side, until medium-rare. (Cook longer if you want burgers more well done.)

3. Place a tomato slice on each of four dinner plates. Top tomatoes with hamburgers. Garnish each with a basil sprig, if desired, and serve.

Makes 4 servings. Per serving: 251 calories, 25 grams protein, 3 grams carbohydrate, 16 grams fat, 79 milligrams cholesterol, 617 milligrams sodium

Jumbo Garden Cheese Burgers

3 pounds lean ground beef
Pepper to taste
8 slices (1 ounce each) semisoft
    cheese with vegetables, or
    Monterey Jack with jalapeno
    peppers
8 whole-wheat hamburger buns, split
Lettuce, arugula or other salad greens
16 thin slices ripe tomato
16 thin slices red onion

1. Prepare barbecue grill or turn on broiler.

2. Shape beef into eight 1-inch-thick patties. Season with pepper.

3. To grill: Put patties directly on grill rack 4 to 6 inches above hot coals. Grill 3 minutes. Turn; grill 5 minutes longer for rare, 8 minutes for medium, 12 minutes for well-done. Top with cheese 2 minutes before burgers are done.

To broil: Broil 4 to 6 inches from heat source 6 minutes per side for rare, 8 minutes for medium, 10 minutes for well-done. Top burgers with cheese and broil 1 minute longer.

4. Put lettuce on buns, top with burgers and tomato and red onion slices. Serve.

Makes 8 servings. Per serving: 551 calories, 42 grams protein, 24 grams carbohydrate, 33 grams fat, 136 milligrams cholesterol, 497 milligrams sodium

Jumbo Garden Cheese Burger

★ SPECIAL—AND WORTH IT

Hamburgers with Creamy Thyme Sauce

Shape these hamburgers like meatballs and then flatten them just slightly during cooking so they cook perfectly.

2 pounds lean ground beef
1 large egg
2 tablespoons Dijon mustard
2 teaspoons minced fresh garlic
½ teaspoon salt
¼ teaspoon pepper
½ cup chopped onion
½ cup white California Zinfandel or
    good-quality rosé wine, or an
    additional ½ cup beef broth
¼ cup beef broth
1 cup heavy cream
1 teaspoon minced fresh thyme leaves
    or ½ teaspoon crumbled dried
    thyme
For garnish: fresh thyme sprigs
    (optional)

1. Mix beef, egg, mustard, garlic, salt and pepper in a large bowl with hands or two forks until blended. Using ¾ cup beef mixture for each, shape into 6 meatballs.

2. Heat a large heavy skillet (not nonstick) over medium-high heat until very hot. Add meatballs. Cook 2 minutes. Turn; flatten to 1-inch thickness; brown second side. Reduce heat to medium. Cook 4 minutes longer for medium-rare. Transfer to a heated platter. Cover loosely with foil to keep warm.

3. Add onion to skillet; cook 5 minutes, stirring often, until golden. Add wine and broth, stirring to scrape up browned bits on bottom of skillet. Bring to a boil. Boil 3 minutes, until half the liquid has evaporated.

4. Add cream; return to a boil. Boil 3 minutes, until thickened. Add minced thyme. Return burgers to skillet and heat.

5. Arrange burgers on platter with some of the sauce spooned on top. Pour remainder into a sauceboat to pass on the side. Garnish with thyme sprigs, if desired, and serve.

Makes 6 servings. Per serving (with wine): 573 calories, 30 grams protein, 4 grams carbohydrate, 48 grams fat, 199 milligrams cholesterol, 395 milligrams sodium

Hamburgers with Creamy Thyme Sauce

Ground Steaks Dijon

Dressy enough for company. Serve steak-style with watercress, crisply fried potatoes and green beans.

1½ pounds lean ground beef
1¼ teaspoons salt
¾ teaspoon pepper
Pinch of granulated sugar
1 tablespoon butter or margarine, at room temperature
2 teaspoons Dijon mustard
½ cup dry white wine or ½ cup chicken broth mixed with ½ teaspoon fresh-squeezed lemon juice
2 tablespoons minced shallot or white part of green onions

1. Mix beef, ¼ teaspoon of the salt, the pepper and sugar in a large bowl with hands or two forks until well blended. Shape into four 1¼-inch-thick patties.

2. Sprinkle remaining 1 teaspoon salt evenly over the bottom of a large heavy skillet. Place skillet over medium heat until hot. Add patties and cook 3 to 4 minutes per side for medium-rare, about 5 minutes per side for medium. (Cook longer if you want meat more well done.) Remove to a heated platter. Cover loosely with a sheet of foil to keep warm.

3. Meanwhile, mix butter and mustard in a small bowl until smooth.

4. Bring wine and shallot to a boil in a small skillet over high heat. Boil 3 to 4 minutes, until reduced to ¼ cup. Remove from heat. Gradually whisk in butter mixture until smooth and slightly thickened.

5. Spoon sauce over patties and serve.

Makes 4 servings. Per serving (with wine): 247 calories, 32 grams protein, 2 grams carbohydrate, 9 grams fat, 101 milligrams cholesterol with butter, 92 milligrams cholesterol with margarine, 680 milligrams sodium

Oriental-Style Burgers

We cut over 300 calories in each of these burgers by replacing some of the beef with vegetables and by tucking them into pita breads instead of buns. For even more crunch in your sandwich, add alfalfa sprouts and sliced cucumber.

12 ounces lean ground beef
3 ounces mushrooms, chopped (about 1 cup)
½ cup chopped green onions
½ cup finely chopped carrot
2 teaspoons soy sauce
½ teaspoon ground ginger
¼ teaspoon garlic powder
Four 4-inch pita breads

1. Mix beef, mushrooms, green onions, carrot, soy sauce, ginger and garlic powder in a large bowl with hands or two forks until well blended. Shape into 4 patties.

2. Heat a large nonstick skillet over medium-high heat. Add burgers and cook 3 to 4 minutes per side for medium. (Cook longer if you want burgers more well done.)

3. Split pitas and serve burgers in pockets.

Makes 4 servings. Per serving: 246 calories, 20 grams protein, 18 grams carbohydrate, 9 grams fat, 54 milligrams cholesterol, 267 milligrams sodium

Pepperburgers with Garlic Potato Spears and Broccoli

The whole dinner is microwaved and served on the same platter to save on cleanup.

1½ **pounds lean ground beef**
3 **tablespoons packaged plain dry bread crumbs**
2½ **teaspoons coarsely ground black pepper**
1 **teaspoon salt, preferably kosher (coarse)**
1 **teaspoon paprika**
1½ **tablespoons minced fresh garlic**
1 **teaspoon olive oil**
2 **large russet potatoes (about 8 ounces each), scrubbed, each cut lengthwise in 8 wedges**
8 **ounces broccoli, separated into 4 equal-size spears**
¼ **cup thinly sliced green onions**

1. Form beef into four 1-inch-thick oval patties.

2. Mix bread crumbs, pepper, salt and paprika on a sheet of waxed paper. Coat patties with crumb mixture, pressing gently so crumbs adhere. Place in the center of a 12-inch round microwave-safe platter.

3. Mix garlic and oil in a medium-size bowl. Add potato wedges and toss to coat evenly. Arrange around patties skin-side toward edge of platter.

4. Place broccoli spears spoke-fashion over potatoes with stem ends toward edge of platter. Sprinkle green onions over all.

5. Cover platter with vented plastic wrap. Microwave on high 8 to 10 minutes, rotating dish ¼ turn twice, until meat is pink in the center and vegetables are almost tender.

6. Let stand 3 to 5 minutes, until vegetables are tender. Drain off juices through vent before uncovering platter. Serve.

Makes 4 servings. Per serving: 506 calories, 35 grams protein, 30 grams carbohydrate, 27 grams fat, 99 milligrams cholesterol, 499 milligrams sodium

Pepperburgers with Garlic Potato Spears and Broccoli

Sauerbraten Burgers

Good accompaniments to these sweet-and-sour burgers are mashed turnips or potatoes, and shredded red cabbage microwaved or cooked stove-top with a little red-wine vinegar and red-currant jelly. Crush the gingersnaps in a blender or a food processor or in a heavy plastic food bag with a rolling pin.

- **1 pound lean ground beef**
- **1 can (8 ounces) tomato sauce**
- **¼ cup finely chopped onion**
- **¼ cup dark raisins**
- **¼ cup fine gingersnap crumbs (from about 4 cookies)**
- **½ teaspoon salt**
- **⅓ cup water**
- **2 tablespoons packed brown sugar**
- **2 tablespoons distilled white vinegar**
- **1 teaspoon Dijon mustard**
- **Pepper to taste**

1. Mix beef, 2 tablespoons of the tomato sauce, the onion, raisins, 2 tablespoons of the gingersnap crumbs and the salt in a large bowl with hands or two forks until well blended. Shape into four ¾-inch-thick patties. Arrange in a 9-inch-square microwave-safe baking dish. Cover loosely with waxed paper.

2. Microwave on high 4 to 6 minutes, rotating dish ¼ turn twice, until patties are firm to the touch and no longer pink. Pour off fat.

3. Mix water, sugar, vinegar, mustard, pepper and remaining tomato sauce and gingersnap crumbs in a medium-size bowl. Pour sauce over patties and cover loosely with waxed paper.

4. Microwave on high 4 to 6 minutes, rotating dish ½ turn and stirring sauce once, until sauce is very hot. Let stand covered 5 minutes.

5. Transfer patties to dinner plates, top with the sauce and serve.

Makes 4 servings. Per serving: 337 calories, 21 grams protein, 24 grams carbohydrate, 17 grams fat, 79 milligrams cholesterol, 747 milligrams sodium

Sauerbraten Burgers

Meatballs

Meatball Stroganoff

Puréeing the seasonings helps distribute them evenly in the ground beef. Serve this dish over egg noodles.

- ¾ **cup diced onion**
- ¼ **cup loosely packed fresh parsley sprigs**
- 1 **large egg**
- 2 **tablespoons water or beef broth**
- ¾ **teaspoon salt**
- ¼ **teaspoon pepper**
- 1 **pound lean ground beef**
- ¼ **cup packaged dry bread crumbs**
- 4 **tablespoons butter or margarine**
- 3 **tablespoons all-purpose flour**
- 1½ **cups beef broth**
- ½ **cup plain yogurt (see Cooking with Yogurt and Sour Cream, page 70)**
- ½ **teaspoon Dijon mustard (optional)**

1. Put half of the onion, the parsley, egg, water, ½ teaspoon of the salt and ⅛ teaspoon of the pepper in a food processor or a blender. Process until smooth, stopping machine once to scrape down sides.

2. Place beef in a large bowl. Add bread crumbs and onion mixture and mix with hands or two forks until well blended.

3. Using 1 heaping tablespoon for each, shape mixture into meatballs.

4. Melt 2 tablespoons of the butter in a large skillet over medium-high heat until foamy. Add half the meatballs and cook about 4 minutes, turning occasionally, until well browned. Remove to a plate with a slotted spoon. Repeat with remaining meatballs.

5. Melt remaining 2 tablespoons butter in the skillet. Stir in remaining onion and cook about 3 minutes, stirring frequently, until tender. Stir in flour and cook 1 minute, stirring constantly.

6. Gradually pour broth into skillet, stirring constantly to blend and to scrape up browned bits on bottom of skillet. Bring to a boil. Reduce heat to low and simmer, stirring frequently, until sauce is thickened.

7. Return meatballs and any juices that have collected on plate to skillet. Simmer 5 minutes, basting meatballs with sauce occasionally.

8. Mix yogurt with mustard in a measuring cup or a small bowl until blended. Stir into sauce. Season with remaining salt and pepper. Remove from heat. Transfer to a large heated bowl and serve.

Makes 4 servings. Per serving: 441 calories, 26 grams protein, 15 grams carbohydrate, 30 grams fat, 187 milligrams cholesterol with butter, 151 milligrams cholesterol with margarine, 962 milligrams sodium

---

Shaping Meatballs

☐ Use a gentle hand when mixing and shaping meatballs; if the meat is packed too tightly or mixed too vigorously, the meatballs will be dry and hard.

☐ Dampen hands with cold water so the meat doesn't stick, and roll mixture lightly between your palms to form fairly smooth balls.

☐ Meatballs may be mixed and shaped ahead of time; in most cases they even improve because the flavors have a chance to blend. Keep them refrigerated until ready to cook. If the meat mixture is very soft, you might want to chill it before shaping so there's less mess.

Swedish Meatballs

1 pound lean ground beef
8 ounces lean ground pork
1 cup packaged plain dry bread crumbs
1 cup milk
¼ cup finely chopped celery
¼ cup finely chopped onion
¼ cup chopped fresh parsley
1 large egg
1 teaspoon minced fresh garlic
1 teaspoon granulated sugar
1 teaspoon salt
¼ teaspoon pepper
4 tablespoons butter or margarine
For garnish: fresh dill sprigs
Creamy Dill Sauce (recipe follows)

1. Mix beef, pork, bread crumbs, milk, celery, onion, parsley, egg, garlic, sugar, salt and pepper in a large bowl with hands or two forks until well blended; mixture will be moist. Using 1 level tablespoon meat mixture for each, shape into 48 meatballs.

2. Melt 2 tablespoons of the butter in a large heavy skillet over medium heat. Add half the meatballs in a single layer. Cook 10 minutes, turning occasionally, until browned and barely pink in the centers. Remove to an ovenproof serving dish with a slotted spoon and cover with foil. Melt remaining 2 tablespoons butter in skillet. Cook remaining meatballs and remove to serving dish.

3. Garnish with dill sprigs and serve with some of the sauce spooned over the top, or cover and refrigerate meatballs to serve later (see Note). Pour remaining sauce into a sauceboat to pass on the side.

Makes 8 servings. Per serving (without sauce): 298 calories, 18 grams protein, 12 grams carbohydrate, 19 grams fat, 101 milligrams cholesterol with butter, 92 milligrams cholesterol with margarine, 455 milligrams sodium

Note: To reheat meatballs: Cover and heat in a 325°F oven about 15 minutes, until warmed through.

Creamy Dill Sauce

3 tablespoons butter or margarine
3 tablespoons all-purpose flour
2 cups beef broth
1 cup sour cream
1 tablespoon snipped fresh dill, or
   to taste
¼ teaspoon grated fresh lemon peel

Swedish Meatballs

1. Melt butter in a small saucepan over medium heat. Stir in flour until frothy. Let bubble 2 minutes, stirring frequently.

2. Gradually stir in beef broth until smooth. Bring to a boil. Reduce heat to low and simmer 10 to 12 minutes, stirring often, until slightly thickened.

3. Stir in sour cream, dill and lemon peel. Remove from heat.

4. Serve sauce immediately or cool, cover and refrigerate. Reheat over medium-low heat 6 to 8 minutes, stirring often, until hot.

Makes 2⅔ cups. Per ⅓ cup: 118 calories, 2 grams protein, 4 grams carbohydrate, 10 grams fat, 32 milligrams cholesterol with butter, 18 milligrams cholesterol with margarine, 263 milligrams sodium

---

Cooking with Yogurt and Sour Cream

Yogurt and sour cream add richness and a pleasant acidic tang to sauces, but they need gentle treatment when heating. Stir yogurt or sour cream into hot sauces as close to the end of cooking time as possible. Never let the sauce boil; heat only to a bare simmer or it will break down and curdle. Remove sauce from the heat as soon as the ingredients are blended; the yogurt or sour cream will continue to heat in the warm sauce.

Hot and Spicy Stir-fried Meatballs with Ginger and Mint

Like many Oriental dishes, the actual cooking is quick and easy—if you have all the ingredients ready first. Serve these meatballs over Japanese soba (buckwheat) noodles, rice or vermicelli.

Meatballs

- 2 tablespoons butter or margarine
- 2 tablespoons minced shallot or white part of green onions
- 1 teaspoon minced fresh garlic, or to taste
- ¼ cup packed fresh mint leaves, chopped
- ¼ cup packaged dry bread crumbs
- 2 tablespoons beef broth or water
- ½ teaspoon salt
- ⅛ teaspoon pepper
- 1 pound lean ground beef
- 2 tablespoons vegetable oil

Sauce

- ⅓ cup thinly sliced green onions
- 1 can (8 ounces) sliced water chestnuts, well drained
- 1 tablespoon minced fresh gingerroot, or to taste
- 1 fresh or canned jalapeño pepper, seeded and chopped (about 1 tablespoon)
- 2 cups beef broth
- ½ cup dry white wine or additional ½ cup beef broth
- 2 tablespoons cornstarch
- ¼ cup soy sauce

1. To prepare meatballs: Melt butter in a large deep heavy skillet or wok over medium heat. Add shallot and garlic. Cook 2 minutes, stirring occasionally, until tender. Stir in mint. Remove from heat.

2. Stir bread crumbs, beef broth, salt and pepper into mint mixture in skillet. Put beef in a medium-size bowl. Add bread-crumb mixture and mix with two forks until blended.

3. Using 2 tablespoons for each, shape meat mixture into 16 meatballs. Put meatballs on a plate. Meatballs will be soft; cover and chill 30 minutes or until firm.

4. To cook meatballs: Heat oil in same skillet or wok over medium-high heat. Add half the meatballs at a time and stir-fry each batch 4 to 5 minutes, until browned. Remove to a bowl with a slotted spoon. Pour all but 2 tablespoons drippings from skillet.

5. To prepare sauce: Add green onions, water chestnuts, gingerroot and jalapeño pepper to skillet. Stir-fry 1 minute.

6. Stir 1 cup of the broth and the wine into vegetables. Bring to a boil. Boil 3 minutes.

7. Meanwhile, mix cornstarch, remaining 1 cup beef broth and soy sauce in a small bowl until smooth. Add to skillet and cook, stirring constantly, until thickened.

8. Stir in meatballs and cook until hot and well coated with sauce.

9. Transfer meatballs and sauce to a large heated bowl and serve.

Makes 4 servings. Per serving (with wine): 396 calories, 25 grams protein, 18 grams carbohydrate, 25 grams fat, 96 milligrams cholesterol with butter, 87 milligrams cholesterol with margarine, 1,537 milligrams sodium

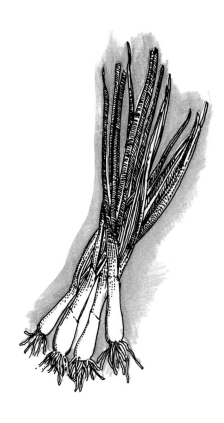

Meat Loaf

Although we give specific proportions for meats in a ground-meat (beef/pork/veal) mixture or have specified all beef, you can use the meat loaf mixture sold in your market. Prepackaged store-wrapped ground meats should be kept in the coldest part of your refrigerator. Cook or wrap tightly and freeze within two days.

To check the seasoning: Cook a small amount of the raw prepared meat mixture in a small lightly oiled skillet. Let cool slightly, then taste seasonings and correct if necessary. Wet hands before shaping loaf so meat doesn't stick. Meat loaves made with pork must be cooked to an internal temperature of 170°F.

Garden Vegetable Meat Loaf

This vegetable-laced meat loaf is delicious fresh from the oven and even better cold the next day with assorted mustards and pickles.

- 2 pounds lean ground beef
- 2 boxes (10 ounces each) frozen chopped broccoli, thawed and drained (see Note)
- 1 cup frozen chopped onion, thawed, or 1 cup fresh
- ⅔ cup quick or old-fashioned oats
- 2 large eggs
- ½ cup milk or water
- 1 envelope (1.5 ounces) meat-loaf seasoning mix

1. Heat oven to 375°F. Lightly grease a 9x5-inch loaf pan.

2. Put all ingredients into a large bowl. Mix with hands or with a sturdy wooden spoon, or beat 3 to 4 minutes with a heavy-duty electric mixer on low speed until well blended. Press mixture into prepared pan.

3. Bake 1 hour, until a meat thermometer inserted in the center registers 160°F. Remove from oven to a wire rack. Cover loosely with foil and let stand 10 to 15 minutes.

4. Drain any juices from pan and turn out meat loaf onto a cutting board. Slice, arrange on a heated platter and serve.

Makes 8 servings. Per serving (with milk): 332 calories, 26 grams protein, 15 grams carbohydrate, 19 grams fat, 142 milligrams cholesterol, 737 milligrams sodium

Note: Thaw broccoli quickly by rinsing with cold water in a strainer.

Cabbage-Lined Meat Loaf

Baking the meat loaf in cabbage leaves is an unusual touch. Serve this with buttered beets or creamed spinach. Heat up plain spaghetti sauce from a jar or a can to spoon over the meat loaf. You can blanch the cabbage leaves and cook the rice ahead. Make this with all ground beef if you prefer.

- 6 very large green cabbage leaves, tough ribs trimmed (see Note)
- 12 ounces lean ground beef
- 10 ounces lean ground pork
- 10 ounces lean ground veal
- 1 envelope (4.6 ounces) beef-flavor rice mix, cooked according to package directions and cooled (2 cups cooked)
- 3 large eggs
- 2 teaspoons prepared mustard
- ½ teaspoon minced fresh garlic

1. Heat oven to 350°F. Grease a 9x5-inch loaf pan.

2. Bring a large pot of water to a boil. Add cabbage leaves and cook just until wilted and pliable. Remove leaves from water and drain on paper towels. When cool, line prepared loaf pan with cabbage, letting leaves hang generously over the sides.

3. Put meats, prepared rice mix, eggs, mustard and garlic in a large bowl. Mix with hands or two forks until well blended. Pack mixture into loaf pan. Fold cabbage leaves over the top of meat and cover with foil.

4. Bake about 1 hour and 20 minutes, until a meat thermometer inserted in the center registers 170°F. Remove from oven and let cool in pan on a wire rack for 20 minutes.

5. Drain any juices from pan and turn meat loaf out onto a heated platter. Slice carefully with a serrated knife. Arrange on platter and serve.

Makes 8 servings. Per serving: 420 calories, 26 grams protein, 23 grams carbohydrate, 25 grams fat, 168 milligrams cholesterol, 798 milligrams sodium

Note: To remove cabbage leaves from the head: Core cabbage and peel off leaves, starting from the core end. Shred remaining cabbage for a cole slaw.

Onion-Topped Meat Loaf

If you prefer, you can make this meat loaf with all ground beef. Serve it with baked potatoes and steamed broccoli or stewed tomatoes.

12 ounces lean ground beef
10 ounces ground veal
10 ounces ground pork
2 large eggs
1½ cups beef broth
½ cup saltine cracker crumbs (from 10 crackers)
1 teaspoon salt
1 teaspoon dried marjoram leaves, crumbled
½ teaspoon pepper
2 large onions, sliced

1. Heat oven to 350°F. Grease a 13x9-inch baking pan.

2. Put meats, eggs, ½ cup of the beef broth, the cracker crumbs, salt, marjoram and pepper in a large bowl. Mix well with hands or two forks.

3. Shape mixture into a 10x4-inch loaf in prepared baking pan. Separate onions into rings and scatter around and over top of meat loaf. Pour remaining 1 cup broth over loaf.

4. Bake about 1 hour and 20 minutes, basting three to four times with pan juices, until a meat thermometer inserted in the center registers 170°F.

5. Remove from oven and transfer to a heated platter or a cutting board. Slice and arrange on platter. Skim fat from pan juices and spoon over meat loaf; serve.

Makes 8 servings. Per serving: 310 calories, 23 grams protein, 7 grams carbohydrate, 21 grams fat, 136 milligrams cholesterol, 421 milligrams sodium

Onion-Topped Meat Loaf

Calorie Counter's Meat Loaf

We replaced some of the beef with ground turkey and used egg whites instead of whole eggs to cut fat and calories. Serve this meat loaf hot or cold on greens with sliced tomatoes and three-bean salad.

> 2 slices day-old white bread, torn in pieces
> ½ cup tomato juice
> 1 pound lean ground beef
> 8 ounces ground turkey
> ¼ cup chopped green bell pepper
> ¼ cup finely chopped onion
> Whites from 2 large eggs
> 1 teaspoon salt
> ½ teaspoon crumbled dried thyme leaves
> ⅛ teaspoon pepper

1. Heat oven to 350°F. Have a large baking pan ready.

2. Mix bread and tomato juice in a large bowl and let stand 5 minutes, until bread is softened.

3. Add beef, turkey, bell pepper, onion, egg whites, salt, thyme and pepper and mix thoroughly with hands, a wooden spoon or a heavy-duty electric mixer.

4. Shape mixture into a 10x4-inch loaf in baking pan.

5. Bake 1 hour, until meat loaf is browned and a meat thermometer inserted in the center registers 170°F.

6. Transfer meat loaf to a heated platter or a cutting board. Cut into slices; arrange on platter and serve.

Makes 6 servings. Per serving: 228 calories, 26 grams protein, 6 grams carbohydrate, 10 grams fat, 75 milligrams cholesterol, 531 milligrams sodium

Miniature Meat Loaves

These meat loaves take less time to cook because of their size. Instead of the potato puffs, you can bake small potatoes along with the meat loaves.

> 1 pound lean ground beef
> ½ cup packaged dry bread crumbs
> 1 small onion, chopped (about ⅓ cup)
> ¼ cup tomato ketchup
> ¼ cup water
> 1 large egg
> 2 tablespoons finely chopped fresh parsley
> ½ teaspoon salt
> ¼ teaspoon pepper
> 2 cups frozen bite-size shredded potato puffs with onions

1. Heat oven to 375°F. Have a shallow baking dish ready.

2. Put beef, bread crumbs, onion, ketchup, water, egg, parsley, salt and pepper in a large bowl. Mix with hands or two forks until well blended.

3. Shape mixture into 4 loaves. Arrange meat loaves and potatoes in baking dish.

4. Bake about 25 minutes, until meat loaves are browned, a meat thermometer registers 160°F when inserted in the center and potatoes are browned and crisp.

5. Transfer meat loaves and potatoes to plates and serve.

Makes 4 servings. Per serving: 511 calories, 25 grams protein, 28 grams carbohydrate, 34 grams fat, 141 milligrams cholesterol, 945 milligrams sodium

Hamburger-Oatmeal Loaf

♥ LOW-CALORIE
Hamburger-Oatmeal Loaf

Serve this comforting meat loaf with buttered boiled cabbage wedges and noodles or mashed potatoes.

- 1 cup old-fashioned or quick-cooking oats
- 1 can (6 ounces) regular or spicy 8-vegetable juice (about ⅔ cup)
- 1 pound lean ground beef
- ½ cup finely chopped onion
- ¼ cup finely chopped green bell pepper
- 1 large egg
- 1 tablespoon finely chopped fresh parsley or celery leaves
- 1½ teaspoons salt
- ½ teaspoon dried sage leaves, crumbled
- ¼ teaspoon pepper
- ¼ cup tomato ketchup

1. Heat oven to 350°F. Lightly grease a shallow 11x7-inch baking dish.

2. Mix oats and vegetable juice in a medium-size bowl. Let stand 10 minutes, until oats are softened and liquid is absorbed.

3. Add beef, onion, bell pepper, egg, parsley, salt, sage and pepper to oat mixture. Mix with hands or with two forks until well blended.

4. Shape meat mixture into a 9-inch-long loaf in prepared baking dish.

5. Bake 45 minutes. Spread with ketchup and bake 10 to 15 minutes longer, until loaf has browned, ketchup is no longer shiny and a meat thermometer inserted in the center registers 160°F. Remove from oven.

6. Let stand 10 minutes. Transfer meat loaf to a cutting board or a heated platter. Slice, arrange on platter and serve.

Makes 6 servings. Per serving: 245 calories, 17 grams protein, 15 grams carbohydrate, 13 grams fat, 83 milligrams cholesterol, 757 milligrams sodium

Grilled Smoky Meat Loaves

Serve with buttered corn or French fries and grilled tomatoes.

1½ cups mesquite or hickory chips,
      soaked in water 1 hour (optional)
  2 large eggs
⅓ cup instant minced onion
  3 tablespoons Worcestershire sauce
  1 cup finely chopped green
      bell pepper
½ teaspoon pepper
  2 pounds lean ground beef
⅔ cup tomato ketchup

1. Prepare barbecue grill or heat oven to 350°F. To prepare barbecue grill: Set an 8-inch-square foil drip pan in the bottom of barbecue. Arrange 30 briquettes around outside of drip pan and light coals. When coals are completely covered with gray ash (about 30 minutes), drain mesquite chips and scatter over coals, if desired.

2. Lightly beat eggs with a fork in a large bowl. Stir in onion and Worcestershire sauce. Let stand 5 minutes, until onion softens. Stir in bell pepper and ground pepper.

3. Add beef to egg mixture and mix with hands or two forks until well blended. Divide mixture in half. Shape each half into a 1¼-inch-thick oval-shape loaf about 6 inches long and 3 inches wide. Spread ⅓ cup ketchup over top of each.

4. To grill: Lightly oil grill over drip pan. Place meat loaves directly on grill rack over drip pan 4 to 6 inches above hot coals. Close grill hood or cover meat loaves with a foil tent. Grill 21 to 26 minutes, until meat is just slightly pink in the center when loaves are tested with a fork.

To bake: Place meat loaves on lightly oiled broiler-pan rack. Bake 21 to 26 minutes, until meat is just slightly pink in the center.

5. Remove meat loaves to a heated platter or a cutting board. Let stand 5 minutes.

6. Slice, arrange on platter and serve.

Makes 6 servings. Per serving: 289 calories, 22 grams protein, 8 grams carbohydrate, 18 grams fat, 140 milligrams cholesterol, 377 milligrams sodium

Country-Style Meat Loaf

Serve this spicy loaf with sautéed bell peppers and onions and mashed potatoes or over toasted Italian bread. Crush the fennel seed with a mortar and pestle, a meat mallet or the bottom of a heavy saucepan.

---

  1 pound sweet Italian sausage,
      removed from casings, broken in
      1-inch chunks
  2 pounds lean ground beef
  3 large eggs
½ cup finely chopped onion
  1 teaspoon salt
  1 teaspoon fennel seed, slightly
      crushed
½ teaspoon pepper

1. Heat oven to 350°F. Have a 9x5-inch loaf pan ready.

2. Cook sausage in a large heavy skillet over medium-high heat, stirring occasionally, until browned and cooked through. Drain in a strainer and let cool slightly.

3. Put cooked sausage, the beef, eggs, onion, salt, fennel seed and pepper in a large bowl. Mix with hands or two forks until well blended. Pack mixture into loaf pan.

4. Bake 1 hour, until a meat thermometer inserted in the center registers 170°F.

5. Turn meat loaf out of pan onto a heated platter. Slice, arrange on platter and serve.

Makes 12 servings. Per serving: 337 calories, 22 grams protein, 2 grams carbohydrate, 26 grams fat, 139 milligrams cholesterol, 560 milligrams sodium

Mexican Meat Loaf with Tomato Sauce

Chopped green chiles add flavor and moisture to the ground beef-and-turkey mixture. Leftovers make excellent sandwiches.

Meat Loaf

1½ cups uncooked oat bran
1 cup finely chopped onion
2 cans (4 ounces each) or 1 can (7 ounces) chopped green chiles, undrained
¾ cup skim milk
½ cup chopped fresh parsley
Whites from 2 large eggs
2 teaspoons salt
1 teaspoon dried oregano leaves
½ teaspoon minced fresh garlic
1 pound lean ground beef
1 pound ground turkey

Tomato Sauce

1 can (15 ounces) tomato sauce
1 tablespoon packed brown sugar
1 teaspoon chili powder
¼ teaspoon ground cumin

1. Heat oven to 350°F. Coat a 9x5-inch loaf pan with no-stick vegetable cooking spray.

2. To prepare meat loaf: Mix oat bran, onion, chiles, milk, parsley, egg whites, salt, oregano and garlic in a large bowl. Add meats and mix with hands or two forks until blended. Pack into prepared loaf pan.

3. Bake 1¼ to 1½ hours, until a meat thermometer inserted in the center registers 170°F. Remove from oven and let cool a few minutes on a wire rack.

4. Meanwhile, stir all Tomato Sauce ingredients in a small saucepan over medium heat until hot and bubbly.

5. Turn meat loaf out onto a cutting board or a heated platter. Slice and arrange on platter. Pour sauce into a sauceboat to pass on the side and serve with meat loaf.

Makes 8 servings. Per serving with ¼ cup sauce: 316 calories, 26 grams protein, 20 grams carbohydrate, 15 grams fat, 80 milligrams cholesterol, 1,019 milligrams sodium

✳ MICROWAVE
Stuffed Meat Loaf Squares

Meat loaf with a savory spinach-and-cheese filling. Serve with spaghetti tossed with butter, sautéed minced garlic, crushed red pepper and parsley.

⅔ cup tomato ketchup
1 large egg
½ cup packaged seasoned dry bread crumbs
1 pound lean ground beef
1 box (10 ounces) frozen chopped spinach, thawed and squeezed dry
¾ cup shredded Monterey Jack cheese (3 ounces)

1. Heat oven to 375°F. Lightly grease an 8-inch-square baking dish.

2. Mix ⅓ cup of the ketchup and the egg in a large bowl. Stir in bread crumbs, then the meat until blended.

3. Pat half of the meat mixture over the bottom of prepared dish. Sprinkle with a layer of spinach, then the cheese. Pat remaining meat mixture on top. Spread with remaining ⅓ cup ketchup.

4. Bake 30 to 35 minutes, until meat is cooked through; check by inserting a small knife in the center. Remove from oven to a wire rack and let cool a few minutes.

5. Cut into squares and serve.

Makes 4 servings. Per serving: 518 calories, 32 grams protein, 24 grams carbohydrate, 33 grams fat, 162 milligrams cholesterol, 879 milligrams sodium

Microwave Method: Prepare and assemble as directed in an 8-inch-square microwave-safe baking dish. Place in oven on a plastic trivet or an inverted microwave-safe plate. Cover loosely with waxed paper. Microwave on high 8 to 10 minutes, rotating dish ½ turn twice. (Meat will be slightly pink.) Let stand covered on flat heatproof surface 10 minutes, until meat is cooked through and pulls away from sides of dish.

Lighter Ground Meat

By combining lean ground beef with ground turkey, you get a flavorful meat mixture with less fat and fewer calories than beef alone. Use our mixture in the following recipes.

Lower-Fat, Lower-Calorie Ground-Meat Mixture

- 12 ounces lean ground beef
- 8 ounces ground turkey
- ½ cup finely chopped onion
- ¼ cup packaged plain dry bread crumbs
- 2 tablespoons finely chopped fresh parsley
- 1 teaspoon minced fresh garlic
- ¾ teaspoon Worcestershire sauce
- ½ teaspoon salt
- ½ teaspoon pepper
- ¼ teaspoon dried thyme leaves
- 3 or 4 drops hot-pepper sauce

1. Mix all ingredients in a medium-size bowl until well blended. Use as recipe directs.

Crispy Meat-and-Potato Bake

Serve this version of shepherd's pie with a lettuce, tomato and green-onion salad lightly dressed with olive oil and vinegar.

- 3 teaspoons olive or vegetable oil
- 1 batch Lower-Fat, Lower-Calorie Ground-Meat Mixture
- 8 ounces mushrooms, sliced (about 2½ cups)
- 1 cup beef broth
- ¼ cup dry red wine or additional beef broth
- 4 teaspoons cornstarch
- 1 box (10 ounces) frozen green peas
- 1 package (15 ounces) frozen hash-brown potato patties, thawed
- 1 medium-size onion, halved and thinly sliced lengthwise (about 1 cup)

1. Heat oven to 425°F. Have a 13x9-inch baking pan ready.

2. Put 2 teaspoons of the oil in a large heavy skillet; swirl to coat bottom and place over high heat. When oil is hot but not smoking, crumble in meat mixture and cook 5 minutes, stirring often to break up chunks, until meat is no longer pink. Reduce heat to medium.

3. Add mushrooms to meat and cook 3 to 5 minutes, stirring often, until mushrooms release their liquid.

4. Mix broth, wine and cornstarch in a 2-cup measure or a small bowl until smooth. Add to meat mixture and cook about 1 minute, stirring constantly, until thickened. Stir in peas. Remove from heat.

5. Scrape meat mixture into baking pan. Crumble potatoes into a medium-size bowl; add onion and mix well. Sprinkle over meat mixture. Drizzle remaining 1 teaspoon oil over top.

6. Bake 10 minutes, then broil 4 to 6 inches from heat source 5 minutes, until onion is crisp-tender and potatoes are browned.

7. Serve from baking pan or spoon onto dinner plates.

Makes 6 servings. Per serving (with additional broth): 340 calories, 25 grams protein, 29 grams carbohydrate, 14 grams fat, 71 milligrams cholesterol, 547 milligrams sodium

Clockwise from top left: Crispy Meat-and-Potato Bake, Tamale Pie, Baked Ziti

Tamale Pie

(Shown on page 78)

Filling

- 2 teaspoons olive or vegetable oil
- 1 batch Lower-Fat, Lower-Calorie Ground-Meat Mixture (recipe, page 79)
- 4 teaspoons chili powder
- 1 can (16 ounces) pinto or red kidney beans, rinsed and drained
- 1 cup 8-vegetable juice
- 1 small red bell pepper, diced (about ½ cup)
- 1 small green bell pepper, diced (about ½ cup)
- ½ cup sliced green onions
- ¼ cup sliced pitted ripe olives
- 3 tablespoons canned chopped green chiles, drained

Crust

- 1 cup yellow cornmeal
- ¾ cup all-purpose flour
- 1 teaspoon baking powder
- ¼ teaspoon baking soda
- ¼ teaspoon salt
- 1 cup plain low-fat yogurt
- 1 large egg
- 1 tablespoon vegetable oil
- ½ cup shredded Monterey Jack cheese (2 ounces)

1. Heat oven to 375°F. Have a shallow 2-quart baking dish ready.

2. To prepare filling: Put oil in a large heavy skillet; swirl to coat the bottom and place over high heat. When oil is hot but not smoking, crumble in meat mixture. Cook 5 minutes, stirring often to break up chunks, until meat is no longer pink.

3. Sprinkle in chili powder and cook 1 minute, stirring constantly. Reduce heat to medium.

4. Stir in pinto beans, vegetable juice, bell peppers, green onions, olives and chiles. Cook about 5 minutes, stirring frequently, until hot. Spoon into baking dish.

5. To prepare crust: Mix cornmeal, flour, baking powder, baking soda and salt in a medium-size bowl.

6. Whisk yogurt, egg and oil in a small bowl until well mixed. Stir into cornmeal mixture just until blended. Stir in cheese. Spread mixture evenly over filling.

7. Bake 30 to 35 minutes, until crust is browned and firm to the touch and a wooden pick inserted in the center comes out clean. If crust browns too quickly, cover with a sheet of foil.

8. Remove from oven to a wire rack and let cool a few minutes before serving.

Makes 6 servings. Per serving: 511 calories, 31 grams protein, 48 grams carbohydrate, 22 grams fat, 121 milligrams cholesterol, 717 milligrams sodium

Baked Ziti

(Shown on page 78)

Lightly sautéed zucchini and yellow summer squash seasoned with dill makes a good accompaniment to this hearty dish.

- 2 teaspoons olive or vegetable oil
- 1 batch Lower-Fat, Lower-Calorie Ground-Meat Mixture (recipe, page 79)
- ¼ teaspoon dried oregano leaves
- ⅛ teaspoon crushed red-pepper flakes
- 1 can (28 ounces) crushed tomatoes in purée
- 1 can (8 ounces) tomato sauce
- ½ cup water
- 8 ounces ziti
- 1 cup shredded part-skim mozzarella cheese (4 ounces)
- 2 tablespoons grated Parmesan cheese

1. Heat oven to 400°F. Have a 13x9-inch baking pan ready.

2. Put oil in a large heavy skillet; swirl to coat bottom and place over high heat. When oil is hot but not smoking, crumble in meat mixture. Cook 5 minutes, stirring often to break up chunks, until meat is no longer pink. Stir in oregano and crushed red pepper and cook 30 seconds.

3. Add crushed tomatoes, tomato sauce and water to skillet and bring to a boil. Reduce heat to low. Cover and simmer 15 minutes, stirring two to three times.

4. Meanwhile, bring a large pot of water to a boil over high heat. Add ziti and cook according to package directions, stirring frequently, until firm to the bite. Drain in a strainer and return to cooking pot.

5. Add meat sauce to drained ziti in pot and stir to mix. Scrape into baking pan and sprinkle cheeses over top. Cover with foil.

6. Bake 10 minutes. Remove foil and bake 5 minutes longer, until lightly browned. Serve from baking pan.

Makes 6 servings. Per serving: 463 calories, 31 grams protein, 45 grams carbohydrate, 18 grams fat, 78 milligrams cholesterol, 875 milligrams sodium

Mediterranean Meat and Eggplant

♥ LOW-CALORIE

Mediterranean Meat and Eggplant

Serve on a bed of noodles.

- 1 medium-size eggplant (about 1 pound), sliced ½-inch thick
- 3 teaspoons olive or vegetable oil
- ⅛ teaspoon pepper
- 1 batch Lower-Fat, Lower-Calorie Ground-Meat Mixture (recipe, page 79)
- ½ teaspoon dried rosemary leaves
- 1¾ cups beef or chicken broth
- 1 box (10 ounces) frozen chopped spinach, thawed and squeezed dry
- 1 jar (7 ounces) roasted red peppers, drained and cut up

1. Remove broiler pan from oven. Turn on broiler.

2. Arrange eggplant slices in a single layer on broiler-pan rack. Lightly brush with 1 teaspoon of the oil and sprinkle with pepper.

3. Broil 4 to 6 inches from heat source 10 to 12 minutes per side, until browned and tender. Remove eggplant to a cutting board; let cool slightly and cut in ½-inch pieces.

4. Put remaining 2 teaspoons oil in a large heavy skillet; swirl to coat bottom and place over high heat. When oil is hot but not smoking, crumble in meat mixture, add rosemary and cook 5 minutes, stirring often to break up chunks, until meat is no longer pink. Reduce heat to medium.

5. Stir in eggplant, broth, spinach and roasted peppers. Cook 5 to 7 minutes, stirring occasionally, until flavor develops, adding a little more broth or water if mixture gets dry.

6. Transfer to a heated platter and serve.

Makes 6 servings. Per serving: 257 calories, 22 grams protein, 11 grams carbohydrate, 15 grams fat, 70 milligrams cholesterol, 536 milligrams sodium

Stir-fried Rice and Meat

Serve a refreshing dessert of sliced fresh pineapple and chilled canned litchi nuts after this main course.

- 2 teaspoons peanut or vegetable oil
- 1 batch Lower-Fat, Lower-Calorie Ground-Meat Mixture (recipe, page 79)
- 1 cup diagonally sliced celery
- 1 tablespoon grated fresh gingerroot or 1½ teaspoons ground ginger
- 1¾ cups chicken broth
- 2 tablespoons cornstarch
- 1 tablespoon plus 1 teaspoon reduced soy sauce
- 3 cups freshly cooked brown or white rice (1 cup uncooked rice simmered in 2 cups water)
- 1 package (6 ounces) frozen Chinese pea pods, partially thawed and separated
- 2 tablespoons rice-wine vinegar
- 1 bunch watercress (about 2 packed cups sprigs), rinsed and dried
- ½ cup diagonally sliced green onions

1. Put oil in a large heavy skillet; swirl to coat bottom and place over high heat. When oil is hot but not smoking, crumble in meat mixture. Cook 5 minutes, stirring often to break up chunks, until meat is no longer pink. Reduce heat to medium.

2. Add celery and gingerroot to meat and cook 2 to 3 minutes, stirring often, until celery is crisp-tender.

3. Meanwhile, mix chicken broth, cornstarch and soy sauce in a 2-cup measure until smooth. Add to skillet with rice and pea pods. Stir-fry 2 to 3 minutes, until sauce is thick and bubbly.

4. Stir in vinegar, then watercress and green onions. Stir-fry about 2 minutes, just until watercress is wilted.

5. Transfer to a large heated bowl and serve.

Makes 6 servings. Per serving: 343 calories, 23 grams protein, 30 grams carbohydrate, 14 grams fat, 70 milligrams cholesterol, 879 milligrams sodium

Stir-fried Rice and Meat

Pita Pocket Burgers

Pita-Pocket Burgers

Sliced fresh seasonal fruits sprinkled with brown sugar makes a refreshing dessert.

Burgers

1 batch Lower-Fat, Lower-Calorie Ground-Meat Mixture (recipe, page 79)
½ teaspoon ground cumin
6 whole-wheat pita breads

Dill Sauce

1½ cups plain low-fat yogurt
2 tablespoons snipped fresh dill or 2 teaspoons dillweed
2½ teaspoons Dijon mustard
1½ teaspoons lemon juice
⅛ teaspoon pepper
Pinch of salt

Vegetables

2 medium-size fresh ripe tomatoes, coarsely chopped (about 1½ cups)
1 medium-size ripe avocado, halved, seeded, peeled and diced (about 1½ cups)
1 cup alfalfa sprouts (about 1½ ounces)
½ cup sliced green pickled peppers (optional)

1. Remove broiler pan from oven and line pan with foil. Turn on broiler.

2. To make burgers: Shape meat mixture into 24 small flat patties and arrange on broiler-pan rack. Sprinkle patties with cumin.

3. Broil (in two batches if necessary) 4 to 5 inches from heat source 4 to 6 minutes without turning, until patties are lightly browned and no longer pink in the centers. While broiling patties, heat pita breads in oven.

4. Meanwhile, make the sauce: Stir all sauce ingredients in a small bowl just until blended.

5. To assemble: Halve warmed pitas crosswise. Fill each half with a spoonful of the tomatoes and avocado, 2 of the burgers, some sprouts and pickled peppers, if desired. Drizzle each with sauce and serve.

Makes 6 servings. Per serving: 366 calories, 23 grams protein, 28 grams carbohydrate, 16 grams fat, 61 milligrams cholesterol, 341 milligrams sodium

One-Dish Meals

Beef Tortini

This easy casserole is like lasagna without the noodles. Look for shredded mozzarella in your supermarket dairy case. Serve with a crisp green salad dressed with a mild garlic vinaigrette, and crusty Italian bread.

- **2 pounds lean ground beef**
- **½ cup coarsely chopped onion**
- **1 can (15 ounces) tomato sauce**
- **1 can (12 ounces) tomato paste**
- **2 boxes (10 ounces each) frozen chopped spinach, thawed and squeezed dry**
- **2 containers (16 ounces each) small-curd cottage cheese**
- **2 cups shredded mozzarella cheese (8 ounces)**
- **8 ounces mushrooms, thinly sliced (about 2 cups), or 1 can (6 ounces) sliced mushrooms, drained**

1. Crumble beef into a large skillet over medium heat. Stir in onion and cook about 8 minutes, stirring often to break up chunks, until beef is no longer pink and onion is tender. Drain off fat.

2. Stir tomato sauce and paste into beef. Bring to a boil. Reduce heat to low and simmer about 20 minutes, stirring occasionally, until slightly thickened. Remove from heat.

3. Meanwhile, heat oven to 325°F. Have a 13x9-inch baking pan ready.

4. Mix spinach and cottage cheese in a medium-size bowl until well blended.

5. Spread one third of the meat mixture in the bottom of baking pan. Layer with half the spinach mixture and half the remaining meat mixture. Repeat layers, ending with meat mixture. Top with mozzarella and mushrooms.

6. Bake 30 minutes, until bubbly and golden brown. Remove from oven to a wire rack. Let stand 10 minutes before cutting and serving.

Makes 10 servings. Per serving: 409 calories, 36 grams protein, 16 grams carbohydrate, 22 grams fat, 96 milligrams cholesterol, 689 milligrams sodium

Beef Tortini

Beef à la Grecque

The rice may be cooked up to two days ahead.

 1 **pound lean ground beef**
 ½ **cup chopped onion**
 ½ **cup chopped green bell pepper**
 2 **teaspoons minced fresh garlic**
 1 **medium-size eggplant (about 1 pound), diced (4 to 5 cups)**
 1 **can (8 ounces) tomato sauce**
 1 **cup beef broth**
 1 **teaspoon salt**
 1 **teaspoon dried marjoram leaves**
 ½ **teaspoon dried rosemary leaves**
 ¼ **teaspoon pepper**
 2 **cups cooked long-grain white rice (⅔ cup uncooked rice simmered in 1⅓ cups water)**
 4 **ounces mozzarella cheese, sliced**

1. Heat oven to 350°F. Have a deep 2-quart baking dish ready.

2. Crumble beef into a Dutch oven over medium heat. Stir in onion, bell pepper and garlic. Cook about 5 minutes, stirring often to break up chunks, until beef is no longer pink and vegetables are crisp-tender.

3. Stir eggplant, tomato sauce, broth, salt, marjoram, rosemary and pepper into beef mixture. Bring to a boil. Reduce heat to medium-low and simmer 10 minutes, until eggplant is tender. Remove from heat.

4. Stir in rice and scrape into baking dish. Top with cheese.

5. Bake 15 to 20 minutes, until casserole is bubbly and cheese is melted and lightly browned. Remove from oven.

6. Serve immediately from baking dish.

Makes 6 servings. Per serving: 372 calories, 21 grams protein, 26 grams carbohydrate, 21 grams fat, 71 milligrams cholesterol, 863 milligrams sodium

Ground Beef and Bulgur

Bulgur—wheat kernels that have been steamed, dried and crushed—is available in grocery health-food sections, in health-food stores or in Middle Eastern specialty shops.

 1 **pound lean ground beef**
 1½ **cups chopped onions**
 1 **teaspoon minced fresh garlic**
 8 **ounces mushrooms, sliced (about 2½ cups)**
 1 **cup medium-grain bulgur**
 1 **can (28 ounces) tomatoes, undrained**
 ½ **cup sliced pitted ripe olives**
 1 **teaspoon dried oregano or basil leaves**
 ½ **teaspoon salt**
Pepper to taste
 1 **cup shredded Monterey Jack cheese (4 ounces)**
 3 **tablespoons chopped fresh parsley**

1. Crumble beef into a large heavy skillet over high heat. Pile onions and garlic on top. When the fat begins to cook out of the meat, combine onions and garlic with beef, stirring to break up large chunks of meat. Add mushrooms and cook, stirring often, until beef is no longer pink and vegetables are tender.

2. Stir in bulgur, tomatoes and olives, cutting tomatoes into the mixture with a spoon. Stir in oregano, salt and pepper and bring to a boil.

3. Reduce heat to low. Cover and simmer 15 minutes, until bulgur is tender. Uncover and simmer until thickened.

4. Sprinkle with cheese and parsley. Cover and cook 3 minutes longer; until cheese melts.

5. Serve from skillet.

Makes 4 servings. Per serving: 653 calories, 35 grams protein, 44 grams carbohydrate, 37 grams fat, 105 milligrams cholesterol, 884 milligrams sodium

Enchilada Stack

✳ MICROWAVE
Enchilada Stack

Serve with a large pitcher of iced tea with lime wedges. To cut calories, substitute a 19-ounce can of drained and mashed pinto or kidney beans for the refried beans.

 1 **pound lean ground beef**
 1 **envelope (1¼ ounces) taco-**
 seasoning mix
 1 **can (16 ounces) refried beans**
 1 **jar (16 ounces) enchilada sauce**
Eighteen 6-inch corn tortillas
 1 **medium-size fresh tomato, cut in**
 ½-inch chunks
 ¾ **cup shredded Cheddar or Monterey**
 Jack cheese (3 ounces)
 4 **cups shredded iceberg lettuce**

1. Crumble beef into a 2-quart microwave-safe bowl lined with two layers of paper towels or into a microwave-safe strainer placed in a microwave-safe bowl.

2. Cover with waxed paper and microwave on high 5 to 6 minutes, stirring once with a fork to

break up large chunks. Discard paper towels or the drippings from bowl.

3. Return beef to bowl; stir in taco-seasoning mix.

4. Put refried beans into a medium-size microwave-safe bowl. Microwave on high 2½ to 3 minutes, stirring once, until hot.

5. Pour enchilada sauce into a 1-quart glass measure. Microwave on high 2 to 3 minutes, stirring once, until hot.

6. For each serving, place 1 tortilla on a microwave-safe dinner plate. Spread tortilla with ⅓ cup of the refried beans and sprinkle with about 2 tablespoons of the tomato. Top with a tortilla, ⅓ cup of the meat mixture, 1 tablespoon of the cheese and ⅔ cup of the lettuce. Cover with another tortilla. Spoon ⅓ cup of sauce over top to cover. Sprinkle with another 1 tablespoon cheese.

7. Microwave uncovered on high 1½ to 2 minutes, until cheese is melted and sauce is bubbly. Serve.

Makes 6 servings. Per serving: 550 calories, 30 grams protein, 66 grams carbohydrate, 19 grams fat, 59 milligrams cholesterol, 1,694 milligrams sodium

Giant Empanadas

Empanadas are Spanish or Mexican turnovers, usually stuffed with a spicy meat-and-vegetable filling. They are good served with shredded lettuce, chopped fresh tomatoes, sour cream and guacamole or a zippy salsa.

1 pound lean ground beef
1 cup chopped onion
1 cup chopped green bell pepper
1 can (14½ ounces) tomatoes, undrained; tomatoes broken up
1 tablespoon chili powder
1 teaspoon ground cumin
1 teaspoon salt
½ teaspoon pepper
2 refrigerated folded piecrusts
Yolk from 1 large egg, mixed with 1 tablespoon water

1. Crumble beef into a large nonstick skillet over high heat. Stir in onion and bell pepper and cook 5 minutes, stirring to break up large chunks of meat, until beef is no longer pink. Drain mixture in a strainer and return to skillet.

2. Stir tomatoes, chili powder, cumin, salt and pepper into skillet and bring to a boil. Reduce heat to low and simmer about 15 minutes, until mixture is slightly thickened. Remove from heat.

3. Meanwhile, heat oven to 400°F. Grease a baking sheet.

4. Place 1 unfolded piecrust at one end of prepared baking sheet. Spoon half of the beef mixture onto one half of pastry round, leaving a 1-inch border at edge. Fold other half of pastry over filling. Press edges to seal. Brush pastry with yolk mixture. Repeat with remaining crust and beef mixture at other end of baking sheet.

5. Bake 20 minutes, until pastry is golden and filling is hot. Remove from oven.

6. Cut each empanada in half and serve.

Makes 4 servings. Per serving: 845 calories, 27 grams protein, 57 grams carbohydrate, 55 grams fat, 138 milligrams cholesterol, 1,335 milligrams sodium

✳ MICROWAVE
Topsy-Turvy Vegetable Beef Pie

8 ounces frozen mixed vegetables (about 2 cups)
2 tablespoons water
⅓ cup tomato ketchup
1 teaspoon prepared mustard
1 large egg
1 pound lean ground beef
½ cup milk
½ cup packaged seasoned dry bread crumbs
¼ teaspoon salt
⅛ teaspoon pepper
2 cups mashed potatoes, at room temperature
3 slices (⅔ ounce each) American cheese, cut in half diagonally

1. Put vegetables and water into a deep 1-quart microwave-safe casserole. Cover with a lid or vented plastic wrap. Microwave on high 3 to 4 minutes, stirring once, until crisp-tender. Remove from oven. Stir in ketchup and mustard.

2. Beat egg in a large bowl. Add beef, milk, crumbs, salt and pepper and mix with hands or a spoon until blended.

3. Press beef mixture over bottom and up sides of a 9-inch microwave-safe pie plate. Cover loosely with waxed paper.

4. Microwave on high 6 to 8 minutes, rotating dish ¼ turn twice, until meat is no longer pink. Remove from oven and carefully drain off fat.

5. To assemble pie: Spread mashed potatoes over meat crust. Top with the vegetable mixture and arrange cheese triangles over top.

6. Microwave uncovered on high 1 to 2 minutes, until cheese is melted.

7. Cut in wedges and serve.

Makes 6 servings. Per serving: 346 calories, 21 grams protein, 25 grams carbohydrate, 18 grams fat, 93 milligrams cholesterol, 927 milligrams sodium

Beef, Spinach and Feta in Pastry

This recipe makes 12 servings, so you can freeze some for another dinner. Wrap the unbaked pies individually in foil and freeze flat. Don't stack until thoroughly frozen. There's no need to thaw before baking; simply place unwrapped pies on a lightly greased baking sheet and bake in a 325°F oven for about an hour, until hot and golden brown.

¼ **cup butter or margarine**
2½ **tablespoons all-purpose flour**
1½ **cups milk**
1 **teaspoon dried rosemary leaves, crumbled**
½ **teaspoon dried thyme leaves**
1 **teaspoon pepper**
2 **pounds lean ground beef**
2 **boxes (10 ounces each) frozen chopped spinach, thawed and squeezed dry**
8 **ounces feta cheese, cut in ¼-inch squares**
2 **cups cooked long-grain white rice (⅔ cup uncooked rice simmered in 1⅓ cups water)**
4 **large eggs**
1 **package (17¼ ounces) frozen puff-pastry sheets, thawed (see Puff Pastry, at right)**

1. Melt butter in a medium-size saucepan over low heat. Stir in flour until smooth and frothy. Let mixture bubble about 3 minutes, stirring often to prevent browning.

2. Gradually stir milk into flour mixture. Increase heat to medium and simmer, stirring constantly, until sauce thickens. Stir in rosemary, thyme and pepper. Remove from heat.

3. Crumble beef into a large skillet over medium heat. Cook about 8 minutes, stirring to break up large chunks, until beef is no longer pink. Drain beef through a strainer to remove fat and transfer to a large bowl.

4. Add spinach, feta cheese, rice and the sauce to beef. Stir until blended.

5. Heat oven to 350°F. Lightly grease two baking sheets.

6. Lightly beat eggs in a medium-size bowl with a wire whisk.

7. On a lightly floured surface, with a floured rolling pin, roll 1 sheet of pastry to a 21x14-inch rectangle. With a sharp knife or a straight-sided pastry wheel, cut pastry into six 7-inch squares. Brush edges of each square with some of the beaten egg.

8. Spoon about ¾ cup of the beef mixture into the center of each pastry square. Gently fold to form a triangle. Press points of pastry together. Press edges with a fork to seal. Brush tops of pies with beaten egg. Repeat procedure with remaining pastry and beef mixture.

9. Arrange pies on prepared baking sheets. Bake 40 minutes, until hot and golden brown. Remove from oven.

10. Arrange pies on dinner plates or a heated platter and serve.

Makes 12 servings. Per serving: 508 calories, 24 grams protein, 28 grams carbohydrate, 33 grams fat, 168 milligrams cholesterol with butter, 156 milligrams cholesterol with margarine, 665 milligrams sodium

---

Puff Pastry

☐ This classic French pastry is delicate, rich and very flaky. Puff pastry is used for fancy pastries such as Napoleons, as a wrapper for savory fillings as in the recipe above, as a potpie crust and for many other delectables.

☐ Making puff pastry is truly an art. Happily, you can avoid this process and purchase it in ready-to-use sheets from your grocer's freezer. The pastry is made by placing bits of chilled butter or other fat between layers of dough, rolling it out, folding it, chilling it and letting it rest. This process is repeated up to eight times. As the pastry bakes, the heat of the oven and the moisture in the butter creates steam which causes the dough to puff and separate into many flaky layers.

☐ To use frozen puff pastry sheets: Thaw, unfold and roll following package directions. Be sure not to let pastry get too warm or it will stretch and not rise properly. If pastry does get warm, slide a baking sheet under it and place in the freezer for a few minutes until chilled and firm.

☐ When cutting unbaked pastry use a sharp knife or pastry wheel and cut firmly to get a clean cut, otherwise, the pastry will stretch and rise unevenly.

Stuffed Golden Bell Peppers

You can cook and refrigerate the rice up to two days ahead. For this dish, choose firm, thick-walled peppers that stand upright.

- 3 tablespoons olive or vegetable oil
- 1¼ cups finely chopped onions
- 1 tablespoon minced fresh garlic
- 8 ounces lean ground beef
- 3 cups cooked long-grain white rice (1 cup uncooked rice simmered in 2 cups water)
- ¼ cup pignoli (pine nuts), toasted (see Note)
- 3 tablespoons chopped fresh parsley
- 1 tablespoon minced fresh thyme leaves or 1 teaspoon dried thyme
- 1 teaspoon minced fresh marjoram leaves or ¼ teaspoon crumbled dried marjoram
- ½ teaspoon salt, or to taste
- 4 large (about 1¾ pounds) golden or red bell peppers
- ¾ cup beef broth

1. Heat oven to 375°F. Have ready a casserole or a baking dish just large enough to hold peppers.

2. Heat oil in a large heavy skillet over medium heat. Add onions and cook 5 minutes, stirring occasionally, until they begin to soften. Stir in garlic and cook 1 minute longer.

3. Crumble ground beef into skillet. Cook, stirring to break up large chunks, until beef is no longer pink. Add rice and stir until coated. Remove from heat.

4. Stir in pignoli, parsley, thyme, marjoram and salt.

5. Slice tops from peppers and reserve. Remove seeds and membranes. Pack rice mixture into peppers and replace tops. Stand peppers upright in casserole. Pour in broth. Cover with a lid or foil.

6. Bake about 40 minutes, until peppers are tender. Serve from the casserole hot or at room temperature.

Makes 4 servings. Per serving: 520 calories, 20 grams protein, 88 grams carbohydrate, 25 grams fat, 40 milligrams cholesterol, 1,045 milligrams sodium

Note: Toast pignoli in a small skillet over medium heat, shaking skillet until nuts are golden brown. Or toast nuts in a small dish in a microwave oven on high.

Micro Stuffed Peppers

Crusty rolls are a good accompaniment.

- 4 large green bell peppers
- ½ cup coarsely chopped onion
- 1 tablespoon vegetable oil
- 2 cans (8 ounces each) tomato sauce
- 1 teaspoon salt
- 1 teaspoon dried basil leaves
- 1 teaspoon dried oregano leaves
- ½ teaspoon minced fresh garlic
- ½ teaspoon pepper
- 1 pound lean ground beef
- 1 cup cooked long-grain white rice (⅓ cup uncooked rice simmered in ⅔ cup water)
- 1 large egg
- 1 teaspoon Worcestershire sauce

1. Cut off tops of peppers. Remove seeds and membranes and discard stems. Finely dice tops (you should have about ¾ cup).

2. Mix diced bell pepper, onion and oil in a 4-cup microwave-safe measure. Cover with vented plastic wrap and microwave on high 3 to 5 minutes, stirring twice, until tender.

3. Stir in tomato sauce, ½ teaspoon of the salt, the basil, oregano, garlic and ¼ teaspoon of the pepper.

4. Mix beef, rice, egg, Worcestershire sauce, remaining ½ teaspoon salt, remaining ¼ teaspoon pepper and 1 cup of the tomato-vegetable sauce in a large bowl until well blended. Spoon into peppers.

5. Spread ½ cup of the sauce in the bottom of a shallow 2-quart microwave-safe casserole. Stand peppers upright in casserole. Spoon remaining sauce over peppers.

6. Cover loosely with a sheet of waxed paper. Microwave on high 20 to 25 minutes, rotating dish ¼ turn three times, until peppers are tender and meat is no longer pink. Let stand covered 5 minutes before serving.

Makes 4 servings. Per serving: 490 calories, 26 grams protein, 30 grams carbohydrate, 29 grams fat, 140 milligrams cholesterol, 1,611 milligrams sodium

Chili

☐ **The Controversy:** Chili, the dish—made from chile, the pods—can arouse more passion and dissent than any other food. Beans or no beans? Tomato sauce or not? Hot or mild? Should you add exotica like cinnamon, ground almonds, wine or raisins? There are hundreds of chili cook-offs annually and three international chili societies, so chili will always be the cause of heated debate. Chili lends itself to experimentation—try some recipes and decide for yourself.

☐ **The Origins:** It is believed that cowboys learned about the dish from the Indians, who sprinkled chiles on their meat before drying it. Not only did the chile beef taste far more exciting than plain beef jerky, but the chiles helped preserve the beef. Tradition says that beans and tomatoes were added to the chile beef to stretch it out toward the end of the trail. The original "Bowl of Red" chili contained only meat.

☐ **A Cool-Headed Guide to Fresh Chiles**: Milder chiles have broader shoulders and blunter tips. The smallest chiles are generally the hottest. Color makes little difference; red chiles are simply sun-ripened green ones. The hottest parts are the seeds and a substance in the ribs called capsaicin. Here's a rundown of some popular varieties:

Ancho Chiles—ripened and dried *chiles poblanos*. Mild in flavor, they are toasted and soaked before using.

California or New Mexico Chiles—medium green; ranging from mild (California) to hot (New Mexico); they're usually steamed or roasted, peeled and seeded. Canned, they're called green chiles and are available whole or chopped.

Chipotle Chiles—dark red in color, these peppers are dried ripened jalapeños. They are very hot, with a distinctive smoky flavor. Purchase them dried or canned in a savory mixture of tomatoes, vinegar, onion and spices labeled *chipotles en adobo.*

Jalapeño Chiles—dark green and about 2½ inches long with a rounded end; extremely hot. They can be found fresh, canned or pickled.

Poblano Chiles—large, shiny, dark-green chiles, mild in flavor. When ripened, they turn a deep red. When ripened and dried, they're called Ancho Chiles.

Serrano Chiles—green when fresh, long, thin and very hot; when dried, they take on a reddish cast. Available canned.

☐ **Mild and Hot Together:** Several varieties of chiles are used together in authentic chili: for the flavor base, a mild chile such as a California; for heat, a Mexican pepper such as jalapeño or serrano; and for spicy sweetness, crushed chile Caribe. People with brave palates add the devilishly hot dried *pequin quebrado*. Most of our recipes use the spice mixture chili powder— powdered chiles mixed with cumin, oregano, garlic and, usually, salt—together with other seasonings and chiles.

☐ **Handling Peppers:** Hot chile peppers can irritate your skin. After working with them, wash your hands with soap and water to remove the oils. If your skin is particularly sensitive, wear rubber gloves. Never touch your eyes while working with chiles.

☐ **Testing the Heat:** To test the intensity of a chile pepper: Taste it very cautiously before adding it to a dish. Even chiles from the same plant can vary in their hotness. Removing the seeds and the ribs from chiles removes some of the heat.

☐ **Putting Out a Fire:** Have at hand bread, rice or other absorbent foods to cool the fire in case you eat too hot a chile. Don't gulp down a cold beverage, which just spreads the heat in your mouth.

☐ **Fixin's and Mixin's:** Offer these crowd-pleasing chili toppers: coarsely shredded Monterey Jack or Cheddar cheese, finely chopped sweet Spanish onion, sliced chile peppers, and sour cream with wedges of lime. A dish of cubed avocados sprinkled with lime juice is refreshing. Midwestern traditionalists opt for spears of dill pickles and raw celery and carrot sticks.

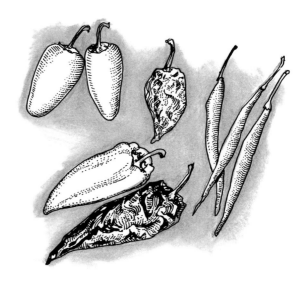

Chipotle Beef

If you can't find chipotle chiles, you can substitute fresh jalapeños: Broil them until charred, wrap in a damp towel, then peel. Corn bread is a perfect accompaniment to this dish.

> 1 **pound lean ground beef**
> ¼ **cup olive oil**
> 2 **cups sliced onions (about 3 medium-size)**
> 4 **dried chipotle peppers, soaked in water until soft, drained and finely chopped (see Chili, page 92)**
> 4 **cups chopped fresh or drained canned tomatoes**
> 3 **cups cooked red kidney beans (8 ounces dried), drained or 2 cans (19 ounces each), rinsed and drained**
> 2 **teaspoons grated fresh orange peel**
> ½ **teaspoon salt, or to taste**
> ½ **cup sour cream**
> 1 **cup sliced red onion**

1. Crumble beef into a large heavy skillet over high heat. Cook meat, stirring often to break up large chunks, until browned. Remove to paper towels with a slotted spoon to drain. Discard fat from skillet.

2. Add oil to skillet and heat over medium heat. Add sliced onions and cook 6 minutes, stirring twice, until wilted. Stir in chipotle peppers, then tomatoes and bring to a boil. Reduce heat to medium-low and simmer 15 minutes, stirring two or three times, until most of tomato liquid has evaporated.

3. Stir in browned beef, the beans and orange peel. Raise heat to medium and simmer until mixture is hot and bubbly. Season with salt and remove from heat.

4. Spoon into bowls and top each with sour cream and red onion and serve.

Makes 4 servings. Per serving: 657 calories, 35 grams protein, 48 grams carbohydrate, 37 grams fat, 89 milligrams cholesterol, 217 milligrams sodium

⏱ MAKE-AHEAD
Three-Bean Chili

A topping of sour cream or plain yogurt mixed with diced cucumber and mint adds a refreshing touch.

> 2 **teaspoons vegetable oil**
> 1½ **pounds lean ground beef**
> 1 **small onion, chopped**
> ½ **teaspoon minced fresh garlic**
> 1 **can (16 ounces) pinto or red kidney beans, rinsed and drained**
> 1 **can (15½ ounces) fava, lima or butter beans, rinsed and drained**
> 1 **can (15½ ounces) chick-peas, rinsed and drained**
> 1 **can (14½ ounces) tomatoes, undrained; tomatoes broken up**
> 1 **can (15 ounces) Spanish-style tomato sauce**
> 2 **tablespoons tomato chili sauce or ketchup**
> 1 **tablespoon dried oregano leaves**
> 1 **tablespoon chili powder, or to taste**
> 1 **teaspoon salt**

1. Heat oil in a Dutch oven over high heat. Crumble in beef; add onion and garlic and cook, stirring to break up large chunks, until beef is no longer pink.

2. Stir in remaining ingredients and bring to a boil. Reduce heat to low. Cover and simmer 1½ hours, stirring occasionally, until meat is tender and flavors have blended.

3. Spoon into bowls and serve.

Makes 8 servings. Per serving: 653 calories, 25 grams protein, 34 grams carbohydrate, 47 grams fat, 58 milligrams cholesterol, 989 milligrams sodium

Texas-Style Ground-Beef Chili with Roasted Red-Pepper Cream

1. Heat oil in a large heavy pot over medium-high heat. Crumble in beef and cook 2 minutes, stirring to break up large chunks. Add onions and garlic and cook 2 minutes, stirring constantly. Drain off fat.

2. Stir broth, wine, tomatoes, tomato paste, chiles and cumin into pot. Bring to a boil. Reduce heat to low. Cover and simmer 1 hour.

3. Uncover and skim off excess fat. Increase heat slightly and cook 15 minutes longer. Remove from heat. Season with salt and stir in chopped cilantro.

4. To serve: Spoon into shallow bowls and garnish each with a spoonful of Roasted Red-Pepper Cream and a sprig of fresh cilantro.

Makes 8 servings. Per serving with 1 tablespoon Roasted Red-Pepper Cream: 571 calories, 44 grams protein, 34 grams carbohydrate, 35 grams fat, 163 milligrams cholesterol, 848 milligrams sodium

Note: Toast the whole ancho chiles in a skillet over medium-high heat or in a 400°F oven, turning several times, for about 4 minutes. Cut open, discard seeds and membranes and soak in hot water 15 minutes. Drain well and chop.

⏱ **MAKE-AHEAD**

★ **SPECIAL—AND WORTH IT**

Texas-Style Ground-Beef Chili with Roasted Red-Pepper Cream

This recipe was developed by Stephan Pyles, chef and co-owner of the Routh Street Cafe in Dallas, Texas, which specializes in southwestern cooking. This makes a big pot of chili, so freeze half (but not the Roasted Red-Pepper Cream) for another day.

1 tablespoon olive or vegetable oil
4 pounds lean ground beef
2 large onions, chopped (about 2 cups)
4 teaspoons minced fresh garlic
2 cups beef broth
1 cup dry red wine or tomato juice
3 large ripe fresh tomatoes, chopped (about 3½ cups)
1 can (6 ounces) tomato paste
2 ancho chiles, prepared and chopped (see Note)
2 chiles serranos or jalapeños, seeded and diced
2 tablespoons ground cumin
2 teaspoons salt, or to taste
3 tablespoons chopped fresh cilantro
Roasted Red-Pepper Cream (recipe follows)
For garnish: fresh cilantro sprigs

Roasted Red-Pepper Cream

2 large red bell peppers
1 cup crème fraîche or sour cream (see Note)

1. Turn on broiler.

2. Put peppers on a baking sheet and broil 4 inches from heat source 10 to 12 minutes, turning several times, until all sides are blistered and have a few dark spots. (You can also blister pepper skins over the flames of a gas burner.) Wrap in a damp towel and let stand 10 minutes.

3. Pull off peel, but do not rinse peppers. Quarter peppers and discard stems and seeds.

4. Process peppers with crème fraîche in a food processor or a blender until smooth.

5. Cover and refrigerate up to 1 week, until ready to use. Use any extra as a dip for raw vegetables.

Makes about 1½ cups. Per tablespoon (with sour cream): 25 calories, 1 gram protein, 1 gram carbohydrate, 2 grams fat, 4 milligrams cholesterol, 7 milligrams sodium

Note: Crème fraîche is a cultured cream found in specialty-food shops; sour cream is a good substitute.

Cincinnati Chili

This cinnamon-scented chili is traditionally served over spaghetti. Top with shredded or chopped American cheese and sliced green onions.

---

2 tablespoons butter or margarine
2 pounds lean ground beef
1 large onion, chopped (about 1 cup)
1 tablespoon minced fresh garlic
Three 2-inch-long bay leaves
2 tablespoons chili powder
1 teaspoon ground cinnamon
1 teaspoon ground allspice
1 teaspoon ground cumin
1 teaspoon dried oregano leaves
1 can (12 ounces) tomato paste
8 cups water
1 teaspoon salt
1 small dried red chile, crushed, or ¼
    teaspoon crushed red-pepper
    flakes, or to taste

1. Melt butter over high heat in a Dutch oven until foamy. Crumble in beef; add onion, garlic and bay leaves and cook, stirring to break up large chunks, until beef is no longer pink.

2. Stir in remaining ingredients. Bring to a boil. Reduce heat to low. Simmer uncovered 3 hours. Remove from heat and discard bay leaves.

3. Spoon into bowls and serve.

Makes 8 servings. Per serving: 378 calories, 22 grams protein, 11 grams carbohydrate, 28 grams fat, 86 milligrams cholesterol with butter, 77 milligrams cholesterol with margarine, 420 milligrams sodium

Vegetable-Meat Chili

Top with shredded cheese, diced avocado and a dollop of sour cream. Serve with hot buttered tortillas. As with most chilis, this is even better the next day.

---

2 tablespoons vegetable oil
2 pounds lean ground beef
2 large onions, coarsely chopped
    (about 2 cups)
1½ teaspoons minced fresh garlic
1 tablespoon ground cumin
1 tablespoon dried oregano leaves
1 tablespoon seeded and chopped
    jalapeño or other hot chile
    pepper
3 cups water
12 ounces mushrooms, quartered
    (about 4 cups)
3 large fresh tomatoes, chopped
1 cup chopped green bell pepper
1 cup chopped red bell pepper
1 cup diced zucchini
½ cup diced celery
½ cup coarsely shredded carrot
2 tablespoons chili powder, or
    to taste
1 teaspoon salt
1 can (16 ounces) red kidney beans,
    rinsed and drained, or 2 cups
    cooked

1. Heat oil over high heat in a large Dutch oven until hot but not smoking. Crumble in beef; add onions and garlic and cook, stirring to break up large chunks, until beef is no longer pink and onions are tender.

2. Add cumin, oregano, jalapeño pepper and water to Dutch oven and bring to a boil.

3. Stir in mushrooms, tomatoes, bell peppers, zucchini, celery, carrot, chili powder and salt. Return to a boil. Reduce heat to low. Cover and simmer 1 hour.

4. Add beans and simmer just until heated through. Remove from heat.

5. Spoon into bowls and serve.

Makes 10 servings. Per serving: 345 calories, 21 grams protein, 15 grams carbohydrate, 22 grams fat, 62 milligrams cholesterol, 300 milligrams sodium

Beef Chili with Zucchini

⏱ **MAKE-AHEAD**
Beef Chili with Zucchini

The chili can be refrigerated up to three days.

- **12 ounces lean ground beef**
- **1½ cups chopped onions**
- **1½ pounds zucchini, cut in small chunks (about 5 cups)**
- **1 can (28 ounces) tomatoes, undrained; tomatoes broken up**
- **1 can (19 ounces) red kidney beans, rinsed and drained**
- **1 can (6 ounces) tomato paste**
- **½ cup water**
- **1 tablespoon chili powder, or to taste**
- **1 teaspoon ground cumin**
- **4 cups freshly cooked long-grain brown rice (1 cup uncooked rice simmered in 2½ cups water)**
- **¾ cup shredded sharp Cheddar cheese (3 ounces)**

For garnish: sliced green onions

1. Heat a Dutch oven over medium-high heat. Crumble in beef and stir in onions. Cook, stirring often to break up large chunks, until beef is no longer pink and onions are nearly tender.

2. Add zucchini, tomatoes, beans, tomato paste, water, chili powder and cumin. Stir gently just until blended. Bring to a boil. Reduce heat to low. Cover and simmer 10 minutes.

3. Uncover chili and simmer 15 minutes longer, stirring occasionally. Remove from heat.

4. Spoon rice into a heated serving bowl or soup plates; top with chili. Sprinkle with cheese and green onions. Serve.

Makes 10 cups, 6 servings. Per serving: 463 calories, 24 grams protein, 59 grams carbohydrate, 15 grams fat, 53 milligrams cholesterol, 709 milligrams sodium

Pumpkin Chili

Pumpkin is an unusual addition to chili, but give this absolutely delicious recipe a try.

- **1 pound lean ground beef**
- **1 can (16 ounces) solid-pack pumpkin**
- **¼ cup chopped onion**
- **1 tablespoon chili powder, or to taste**
- **2 cans (16 ounces each) stewed tomatoes, undrained**
- **1 teaspoon salt**
- **1 can (16 ounces) red kidney beans, undrained**

1. Crumble beef into a large heavy saucepan over medium heat. Cook, stirring to break up large chunks, until beef is no longer pink.

2. Stir pumpkin, onion and chili powder into saucepan and cook 5 minutes, stirring frequently.

3. Add tomatoes and salt and bring to a boil. Reduce heat to low. Cover and simmer 20 minutes, stirring occasionally.

4. Add beans and their liquid and simmer uncovered 20 minutes longer, stirring occasionally, until chili has thickened. Remove from heat.

5. Spoon chili into bowls and serve.

Makes 6 servings. Per serving: 334 calories, 20 grams protein, 26 grams carbohydrate, 17 grams fat, 51 milligrams cholesterol, 619 milligrams sodium

Patchwork Chili

Green tomatoes add a pleasantly tart flavor to this chili. Top with yogurt mixed with green or ripe pitted olives and *peperoncini*, hot little peppers that come in a jar.

- **1 pound lean ground beef**
- **½ cup chopped onion**
- **3 medium-size green tomatoes (about 1 pound), chopped**
- **1 can (16 ounces) red kidney beans, undrained**
- **1 can (15 ounces) chick-peas, undrained**
- **1 medium-size green bell pepper, chopped**
- **1 can (6 ounces) tomato paste**
- **⅓ cup water**
- **1 teaspoon chili powder, or to taste**
- **½ teaspoon ground cumin**
- **½ teaspoon salt**
- **⅛ teaspoon ground red pepper**

1. Crumble beef into a Dutch oven over medium heat. Cook, stirring to break up large chunks, until beef is no longer pink.

2. Stir in remaining ingredients and bring to a boil. Reduce heat to low. Cover; simmer 1 hour, stirring occasionally, until chili is thickened.

3. Spoon into bowls and serve.

Makes 6 servings. Per serving: 342 calories, 23 grams protein, 34 grams carbohydrate, 13 grams fat, 51 milligrams cholesterol, 235 milligrams sodium

Lamb

From legs to chops to ground, from company-fancy to everyday-delicious, the recipes that follow will show off your cooking skills whether you're the family gourmet, the weekend chef or a newcomer to the kitchen.

Roast Leg of Lamb with Pan Gravy; Steamed Baby
Artichokes

Leg of Lamb

☐ **Tasty Options:** A whole bone-in leg of lamb can weigh anywhere from 6 to 11 pounds. You can buy half—either the shank end or the sirloin or butt end. The shank end is meatier, has less fat and is easier to carve; you can recognize it by the protruding leg bone. Leg of lamb is also sold boned, after which it is rolled and tied or butterflied (spread out flat). Before cooking, cut off all of the thin papery membrane (called the fell) along with any excess fat.

☐ **As You Like It:** Lamb is a red meat, so it's at its best roasted rare to medium-rare, but if you like your beef more on the medium- to well-done side, you'll want to cook lamb a little longer too. Properly cooked lamb is juicy and succulent.

☐ **Standing Time:** As the meat rests, the juices redistribute throughout and the temperature rises 5 to 10 degrees depending on the size of the cut. After standing, the lamb will be evenly cooked, juicy and done to a turn. Unless directed otherwise, cover the meat loosely with a foil tent or a sheet of foil while it stands. Never cover the meat tightly because it will steam.

☐ **Lamb Roasting Chart:** These estimated cooking times are based on meat roasting in a 325°F oven. Remove the roast when the meat thermometer inserted in the thickest part, not touching bone, registers 5 to 10 degrees below desired doneness temperature. Because of the heat retained in the meat, the internal temperature will continue to rise after the roast is removed from the oven. Take out small cuts of lamb when the internal temperature is 5 degrees below desired serving temperature, larger roasts when the internal temperature is 10 degrees below desired serving temperature. Like any roast, leg of lamb needs standing time out of the oven.

Cut	Weight in lbs.	Temperature	Minutes per lb.
Leg, Bone-in	5–7	140°F (rare)	17–20
		150°F (medium)	21–24
		160°F (medium-well)	24–27
Leg, Bone-in	7–9	140°F (rare)	13–15
		150°F (medium)	16–18
		160°F (medium-well)	18–20
Leg, Boneless, Rolled, Tied	4–7	140°F (rare)	25–29
		150°F (medium)	29–32
		160°F (medium-well)	32–34

Source: The American Lamb Council

★ SPECIAL—AND WORTH IT
♥ LOW-CALORIE

Roast Leg of Lamb with Pan Gravy

Lemon, garlic and oregano complement a leg of lamb perfectly. Estimate 13 to 15 minutes per pound cooking time for rare meat. Roast small new potatoes with the meat for the last hour. Serve with Steamed Baby Artichokes (recipe follows), cooked and buttered frozen baby corn and sugar-snap peas, and a mixed green salad with a vinaigrette dressing.

1 tablespoon finely minced fresh garlic
  (from 3 large cloves)
1 tablespoon chopped fresh oregano
  leaves or 2 teaspoons dried
  oregano
½ teaspoon salt
⅓ cup fresh-squeezed lemon juice
One 8½-pound bone-in leg of lamb,
  trimmed of excess fat
2 teaspoons vegetable oil
Pan Gravy (recipe follows)
For garnish: fresh oregano sprigs
  (optional)

1. Heat oven to 350°F. Have ready a large roasting pan with a rack.

2. Mix garlic, oregano, salt and 2 teaspoons of the lemon juice with a fork in a small bowl until blended.

3. Make 6 to 8 deep cuts in meat near the bone with a small knife. Push some of the garlic mixture into each cut with a small spoon. Rub surface with remaining mixture, then the oil. Place roast on rack in pan.

4. Roast lamb 1¾ to 2¼ hours, basting four times with remaining lemon juice, to desired doneness (for rare: 130°F on a meat thermometer inserted in thickest part, not touching bone; 140°F for medium; 150°F for medium-well).

5. Remove lamb to a cutting board. Cover with a loose foil tent to keep warm. Let stand 10 minutes; internal temperature should rise about 10 degrees. Meanwhile, make the gravy from pan juices.

6. Carve meat in thin slices (see Carving a Bone-in Leg of Lamb, at right). Arrange on a heated platter and garnish with oregano sprigs, if desired. Serve with Pan Gravy on the side.

Makes 12 servings meat with leftovers. Per 4-ounce serving (without gravy): 211 calories, 32 grams protein, 0 grams carbohydrate, 8 grams fat, 113 milligrams cholesterol, 106 milligrams sodium

Pan Gravy

Pan juices from roast leg of lamb
2 tablespoons all-purpose flour
¼ teaspoon pepper
2 cups water or beef broth

1. Spoon off and discard all but 2 tablespoons fat from juices in roasting pan. Sprinkle in flour and pepper.

2. Place roasting pan over medium-high heat. Stir flour mixture until smooth, scraping up browned bits on bottom of pan.

3. Gradually whisk in water until blended. Bring to a boil. Reduce heat to low and simmer 5 minutes, stirring two or three times, until gravy is thickened. Pour into a sauceboat and serve with the lamb.

Makes 2 cups. Per tablespoon (with water): 9 calories, 0 grams protein, 0 grams carbohydrate, 1 gram fat, 1 milligram cholesterol, 17 milligrams sodium

⏱ MAKE-AHEAD
✳ MICROWAVE
Steamed Baby Artichokes

You can prepare artichokes for cooking early in the day. Just be sure to refrigerate in a bowl of cold water and ¼ cup lemon juice to prevent browning.

2 pounds (16 to 18) baby artichokes
Water
2 tablespoons lemon juice
½ teaspoon salt
For garnish: lemon wedges

1. Discard tough outer leaves from artichokes, leaving the tender lighter-colored ones. Trim stems. Quarter medium-size artichokes or halve small ones. Remove the fuzzy chokes with a teaspoon.

2. Put artichokes in a large deep skillet. Add 2 inches of water, lemon juice and salt. Bring to a boil over high heat. Reduce heat to medium and simmer uncovered 12 to 15 minutes, until stem ends are fork-tender.

3. Drain artichokes and serve hot with lemon wedges.

Makes 12 servings. Per serving: 15 calories, 1 gram protein, 4 grams carbohydrate, 0 grams fat, 0 milligrams cholesterol, 24 milligrams sodium

Microwave Method: Trim and cut artichokes as directed. Place in a round shallow microwave-safe casserole. Sprinkle with 2 tablespoons lemon juice; add ¼ cup water and a dash of salt. Cover with a lid or vented plastic wrap. Microwave on high 7 to 10 minutes, stirring twice, until stem ends are almost tender. Let stand 3 minutes until tender; drain and serve.

Carving a Bone-in Leg of Lamb

☐ With lower leg bone to the right, remove two or three lengthwise slices from the thin side to form a solid base for the roast to rest on.

☐ Turn roast on its base. Starting at the shank end, remove a small wedge cut. Then make perpendicular slices toward the leg bone.

☐ Release slices by cutting under them and along the leg bone, starting at the shank end. Lift slices to serving dish.

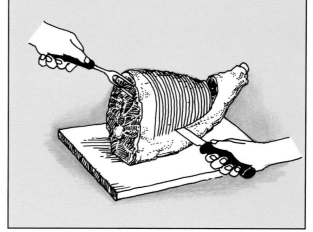

Garlic-Roast Leg of Lamb

♥ LOW-CALORIE
Garlic-Roast Leg of Lamb

The sherry adds a delicate, slightly sweet flavor to the gravy.

2 **cups vegetables from gravy, sautéed**
    (see Best-Ever Gravy, page 10)
One **8½-pound leg of lamb, trimmed of**
    excess fat
2 **medium-size cloves garlic, each cut**
    in 6 slivers
1 **teaspoon dried rosemary leaves**
⅛ **teaspoon salt**
⅛ **teaspoon pepper**
1 **teaspoon vegetable oil**
1 **cup dry sherry wine or water**
Best-Ever Gravy (recipe, page 10)

1. Heat oven to 350°F. Have ready a large roasting pan with the sautéed vegetables.

2. Make deep cuts in the roast with a small knife in 6 to 8 places near the bone and push a sliver of garlic into each one.

3. Mix remaining garlic slivers with rosemary, salt and pepper and rub over surface of roast. Rub roast with oil.

4. Place roast on the vegetables in roasting pan and sprinkle with most of the sherry.

5. Roast 1¾ to 2½ hours, basting three or four times with the remaining sherry, to desired doneness (for rare: 130°F on a meat thermometer inserted in thickest part, not touching bone; 140°F for medium; 150°F for medium-well).

6. Remove lamb to a cutting board and cover with a loose foil tent. Let stand 10 to 15 minutes; internal temperature should rise about 10 degrees. Meanwhile, make the gravy from pan juices.

7. Cut meat in thin slices (see Carving a Bone-in Leg of Lamb, page 101). Arrange on a heated platter. Serve with Best-Ever Gravy on the side.

Makes 12 servings meat with leftovers, ⅔ cup gravy.
Per 4-ounce serving with 2 tablespoons gravy (with water and oil): 239 calories, 33 grams protein, 2 grams carbohydrate, 10 grams fat, 114 milligrams cholesterol, 136 milligrams sodium

Speedy Leg of Lamb with Herb Crust

For medium-rare meat, allow 9 to 10 minutes cooking time per pound; for medium-well, add an additional 45 to 60 seconds per pound. This goes well with French Peas, and Potatoes with Garlic and Lemon (recipes follow).

⅓ cup packaged plain dry bread crumbs
2 tablespoons dried parsley flakes
½ teaspoon dried thyme leaves,
    crumbled
½ teaspoon dried marjoram leaves,
    crumbled
½ teaspoon dried sage leaves, crumbled
¼ teaspoon salt
¼ teaspoon pepper
2 tablespoons Dijon mustard mixed
    with 2 teaspoons minced fresh
    garlic
One 4-pound bone-in shank portion
    leg of lamb, trimmed of excess fat

1. Mix crumbs, herbs, salt and pepper on a sheet of waxed paper or in a small bowl. Brush mustard mixture all over lamb. Sprinkle lamb with crumb mixture, pressing crumbs gently into mustard.

2. To prevent overcooking: Wrap 2 inches of the shank end with a smooth layer of foil. Mold a 1¼-inch-wide strip of foil around top and sides of cut edge (see Using Foil in the Microwave, page 8).

3. Place lamb meaty-side up on a microwave-safe roasting rack with sides or a 13x9-inch microwave-safe baking dish. Insert a microwave-safe meat thermometer, if you have one, in thickest part of meat, not touching bone.

4. Microwave uncovered on medium 28 minutes, rotating dish ½ turn twice. Remove foil.

5. Microwave 8 to 12 minutes longer, until temperature registers 130°F for rare. Transfer roast to a cutting board.

6. Let stand uncovered 15 minutes, until internal temperature reaches 140°F. Lamb will be pink in the center and crumb coating dry.

7. Cut lamb in thin slices. Arrange on a heated platter and serve.

Makes 8 servings. Per 4-ounce serving: 331 calories, 29 grams protein, 3 grams carbohydrate, 21 grams fat, 110 milligrams cholesterol, 216 milligrams sodium

French Peas

1 bag (20 ounces) frozen green peas
    (4 cups)
4 loosely packed cups shredded
    iceberg lettuce (8 ounces)
2 tablespoons butter or margarine
½ teaspoon salt
⅛ teaspoon pepper

1. Mix all ingredients in a 2-quart microwave-safe bowl. Cover with a lid or vented plastic wrap.

2. Microwave on high 6 to 7 minutes, stirring twice, until peas are hot and lettuce is crisp-tender. Let stand covered 2 minutes; serve.

Makes 8 servings. Per serving: 81 calories, 4 grams protein, 10 grams carbohydrate, 3 grams fat, 9 milligrams cholesterol with butter, 0 milligrams cholesterol with margarine, 262 milligrams sodium

New Potatoes with Garlic and Lemon

16 small new potatoes, scrubbed (about
    3 pounds)
2 tablespoons olive oil
1 tablespoon lemon juice
½ teaspoon minced fresh garlic
½ teaspoon salt
¼ teaspoon pepper

1. Cut a ¾-inch-wide strip of peel from around center of each potato.

2. Mix olive oil, lemon juice, garlic, salt and pepper in a shallow 3-quart microwave-safe baking dish. Add potatoes and stir to coat.

3. Cover with a lid or vented plastic wrap. Microwave on high 12 to 14 minutes, stirring twice, until potatoes are almost tender. Let stand covered 3 minutes, until tender, before serving.

Makes 8 servings. Per serving: 120 calories, 2 grams protein, 20 grams carbohydrate, 3 grams fat, 0 milligrams cholesterol, 137 milligrams sodium

Grilled Rolled Leg of Lamb with Garlic and Jalapeños

This recipe comes from a reader in central Texas who says that barbecue in her area has its own distinct flavor: It's not sweet and has a fiery accent in both basting and serving sauces. This meat is especially delicious grilled over chips of mesquite.

Lamb

One 3- to 4-pound boneless leg of lamb, trimmed of all visible fat, rolled and tied
4 cloves garlic, each cut in 4 slivers
1 small fresh or canned jalapeño pepper, seeded and cut in 16 slivers

Basting Sauce

1 cup water
½ cup cider vinegar
½ cup dry red wine
¼ cup butter or margarine
1 large clove garlic, peeled and crushed with the flat side of a heavy chef's knife
1 teaspoon salt
1 teaspoon pepper

1. To prepare lamb: Make sixteen ½-inch-deep slits with the tip of a small knife all over roast and push a sliver of garlic and jalapeño pepper into each.

2. Prepare barbecue grill or turn on broiler.

3. To make basting sauce: Put water, vinegar, wine, butter, garlic, salt and pepper in a small saucepan (not uncoated aluminum). Heat over medium heat until hot.

4. To grill: Place lamb directly on grill rack 4 to 6 inches above hot coals. Place sauce on edge of grill to keep hot while basting meat. Grill roast about 35 to 40 minutes, turning and basting with sauce four times, until a meat thermometer inserted in thickest part registers 130°F for rare. (Grill longer if you want lamb more well done.)

To broil: Place lamb on broiler-pan rack. Broil 4 to 5 inches from heat source 35 to 40 minutes, turning roast and basting as directed, until a meat thermometer inserted in thickest part registers 130°F for rare.

5. Transfer roast to a cutting board. Cover loosely with a sheet of foil and let stand 15 minutes; internal temperature should rise to 140°F. Carve lamb in thin slices and arrange on a heated platter. Bring leftover basting sauce to a boil and pour into a sauceboat to pass on the side.

Makes 8 servings with leftovers. Per 4-ounce serving: 250 calories, 32 grams protein, 1 gram carbohydrate, 12 grams fat, 125 milligrams cholesterol with butter, 113 milligrams cholesterol with margarine, 305 milligrams sodium

---

Grilling Tips

☐ **How Hot?:** Start a charcoal fire 30 to 40 minutes before cooking. Here's how to determine the temperature of the fire on an open grill:

Very Hot (450°–500°F): Coals should be glowing with some gray ash around the edges.

Hot (400°–450°F): Coals are covered with gray ash; you can hold your hand over coals at cooking height for 2 to 3 seconds.

Medium (350°–400°F): You can hold your hand over coals for 4 seconds.

Low (300°–350°F): You can hold your hand over coals for 5 to 6 seconds.

To determine the heat of a closed grill: Set an oven thermometer inside at cooking height.

☐ **Barbecue Safety:** Make sure your grill is located on a flat, level surface, away from overhangs and fences that could be ignited. Never use gasoline or kerosene as a fire starter, and never, never add lighter fluid directly to hot coals. Instead, to give spark to a sluggish fire, soak a few briquettes in lighter fluid in a small metal container for a few seconds, add to coals and light. Don't cover a charcoal grill until you are ready to cook. Covering the grill might put out the fire or prevent lighter fluid from being completely burned off, giving food an off taste.

☐ **Ready Yet?:** Cooking times given in recipes are approximate and should be used only as guides. Outdoor temperature, wind and type of grill all make a difference. Check food often for best results.

☐ **Gas Grills:** Our grilling instructions are for cooking over charcoal. When using a gas grill, follow manufacturer's directions for using drip pans and arranging lava rocks.

Rolled Leg of Lamb with Fresh Tomato Sauce

The Fresh Tomato Sauce may be prepared up to two days before serving.

One 3- to 4-pound boneless leg of lamb,
      trimmed of all visible fat
3 tablespoons olive or vegetable oil
1 tablespoon chopped fresh rosemary
      leaves or 1½ teaspoons dried
      rosemary, crumbled
2 teaspoons minced fresh garlic
1 teaspoon salt
½ teaspoon pepper
Fresh Tomato Sauce (recipe follows)

1. On a flat surface, open meat flat like a book with a long side nearest you. Brush with half the oil; sprinkle with rosemary, garlic and half each of the salt and pepper. Starting from a long side, roll up meat like a jelly roll. Tie roast with white string at 1-inch intervals.

2. Prepare barbecue grill or turn on broiler.

3. Brush roast with remaining 1½ tablespoons oil, sprinkle with remaining ½ teaspoon salt and ¼ teaspoon pepper.

4. To grill: Place roast directly on grill rack 4 to 6 inches above hot coals. Grill about 35 minutes, turning four times, until a meat thermometer inserted in thickest part registers 130°F for rare. (Grill longer if you want lamb more well done.)

To broil: Place lamb on broiler-pan rack. Broil 4 to 5 inches from heat source about 35 minutes, turning four times, until done as desired.

5. Transfer roast to a cutting board. Cover loosely with a sheet of foil and let stand 15 minutes; internal temperature should rise 10 degrees.

6. Remove strings from roast and cut in thin slices. Arrange on a heated platter. Serve with Fresh Tomato Sauce on the side.

Makes 8 servings meat with leftovers. Per 4-ounce serving (without sauce): 240 calories, 32 grams protein, 0 grams carbohydrate, 11 grams fat, 113 milligrams cholesterol, 258 milligrams sodium

Fresh Tomato Sauce

4 tablespoons butter or margarine
2 large shallots, minced (about ¼ cup),
      or ¼ cups minced green onions,
      white part only
2 pounds firm-ripe fresh tomatoes,
      peeled, seeded and chopped (about
      3 cups)
½ teaspoon salt
¼ teaspoon pepper
¼ cup dry white wine or chicken broth
¼ cup chopped fresh basil leaves
      or parsley

1. Melt 2 tablespoons of the butter in a medium-size saucepan (not uncoated aluminum) over medium-high heat. Add shallots and cook 3 to 4 minutes, stirring constantly, until tender.

2. Add tomatoes, salt and pepper to saucepan. Reduce heat to medium and cook 5 to 8 minutes, stirring occasionally, until tomatoes release their liquid.

3. Stir in wine and bring to a simmer. Simmer 15 minutes, until sauce is thick. (If making sauce ahead, cover and refrigerate now; see Note.)

4. Add remaining 2 tablespoons butter and the basil; stir just until butter melts in. Serve hot with the lamb.

Makes 2 cups. Per ¼ cup sauce (with wine): 76 calories, 1 gram protein, 5 grams carbohydrate, 6 grams fat, 18 milligrams cholesterol with butter, 0 milligrams cholesterol with margarine, 207 milligrams sodium

Note: Tomato sauce may be prepared up to two days ahead, but don't add the remaining butter and basil, until reheating.

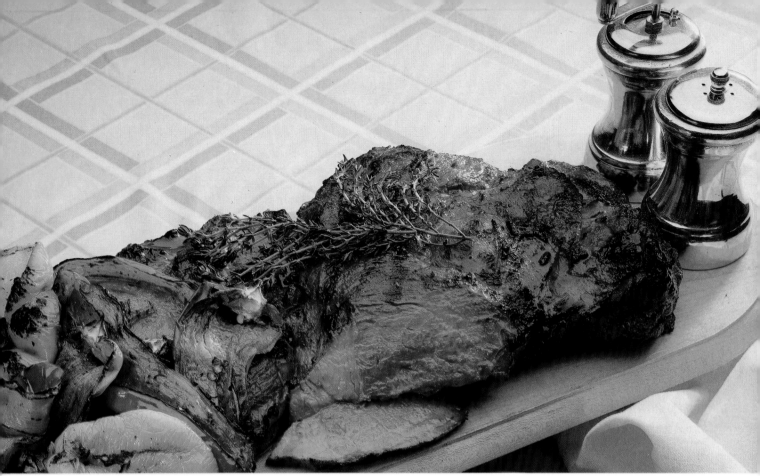

Grilled Butterflied Leg of Lamb with Coriander and Garlic

Grilled Butterflied Leg of Lamb with Coriander and Garlic

The beauty of a grilled butterflied leg of lamb is that it offers meat cooked to all tastes. When the center is medium-rare, the ends are crisp and well done. Serve the lamb with seeded halved bell or frying peppers: Brush them with Italian dressing and grill or broil about 10 minutes, turning and basting once, until lightly charred and tender.

- ½ **cup red-currant jelly, melted**
- ½ **cup fresh-squeezed lemon juice**
- 3 **tablespoons olive oil**
- 1½ **tablespoons salt**
- 4 **teaspoons ground coriander seed**
- 4 or 5 **small cloves garlic, crushed**
- 1 **teaspoon pepper**

One 3- to 4-pound boneless leg of lamb, trimmed of all visible fat and butterflied

1. Mix jelly, lemon juice, oil, salt, coriander, garlic and pepper in a large bowl.

2. Add lamb to jelly mixture and turn to coat. Cover and marinate in refrigerator at least 8 hours or up to 2 days, turning several times.

3. Prepare barbecue grill or turn on broiler.

4. Drain lamb; discard marinade.

5. To grill: Open up lamb and place flat directly on grill rack 4 to 6 inches above hot coals. Grill 10 to 15 minutes per side, depending on thickness, until a meat thermometer inserted in thickest part registers 135°F for rare. (Grill longer if you want meat more well done.)

To broil: Lay lamb flat on broiler-pan rack. Broil 4 to 5 inches from heat source 10 to 15 minutes per side depending on thickness, until a meat thermometer inserted in thickest part registers 135°F for rare.

6. Transfer lamb to a cutting board and cover loosely with a sheet of foil. Let stand 10 minutes; internal temperature should rise 5 degrees. Carve in thin slices, arrange on a heated platter and serve.

Makes 8 servings. Per serving: 235 calories, 33 grams protein, 3 grams carbohydrate, 9 grams fat, 116 milligrams cholesterol, 329 milligrams sodium

Planned-overs

Curried Lamb with Fruit

A deliciously spicy way with leftover lamb. Serve over steamed rice or couscous.

3 tablespoons curry powder
1 tablespoon all-purpose flour
1 teaspoon salt
2 cups well-trimmed cubed
   cooked lamb
2 tablespoons vegetable oil
1 tablespoon butter or margarine
1 large onion, sliced
1 large tart apple, peeled and cut in
   small chunks
1 cup chicken broth
1 can (8½ ounces) pineapple chunks
   in juice, drained
½ cup mango chutney

1. Mix 2 tablespoons of the curry powder, the flour and salt in a medium-size bowl. Add lamb and toss to coat.

2. Heat oil and butter in a large skillet over medium-high heat until butter melts. Add lamb mixture and cook 5 minutes, stirring often. Transfer lamb to a bowl with a slotted spoon.

3. Add onion, apple and remaining 1 tablespoon curry powder to skillet. Cook 5 minutes, stirring often, until onion is tender.

4. Add chicken broth and stir to scrape up browned bits on bottom of skillet. Bring to a boil. Reduce heat to low and simmer 3 minutes, until sauce has thickened slightly. Stir in pineapple chunks, chutney and the lamb and cook just until hot.

5. Transfer to a medium-size heated bowl and serve.

Makes 4 servings. Per serving: 385 calories, 22 grams protein, 42 grams carbohydrate, 16 grams fat, 83 milligrams cholesterol with butter, 74 milligrams cholesterol with margarine, 867 milligrams sodium

Lamb Fricassee with Vegetables

Serve over freshly cooked rice, barley or couscous. Make this fricassee with leftover gravy or substitute store-bought gravy from a can or a mix.

2 tablespoons vegetable oil
2 cups well-trimmed cubed
   cooked lamb
1 medium-size onion, chopped
2 cloves garlic, minced
1 box (10 ounces) frozen green peas
1½ cups brown gravy
2 teaspoons dried rosemary leaves,
   crushed
½ teaspoon salt
Pepper to taste
⅓ cup minced fresh parsley

1. Heat oil in a large skillet over medium-high heat. Add lamb, onion and garlic and cook about 5 minutes, stirring frequently, until onion is tender but not browned.

2. Add peas to lamb mixture. Stir in gravy, rosemary, salt and pepper. Bring to a boil. Reduce heat to low and simmer about 3 minutes, until lamb and peas are hot. Remove from heat.

3. Serve from skillet or transfer to a medium-size heated serving dish. Sprinkle with parsley and serve.

Makes 4 servings. Per serving: 567 calories, 24 grams protein, 22 grams carbohydrate, 41 grams fat, 132 milligrams cholesterol, 1,201 milligrams sodium

Lamb with Spinach and Yogurt

Serve over rice cooked in chicken broth with a pinch of ground turmeric or a few filaments of saffron to give it a yellow color and a very special flavor.

- **2 tablespoons butter or margarine**
- **½ cup chopped onion**
- **1 tablespoon mild curry powder**
- **12 ounces well-trimmed cooked lamb, cut in ¾-inch cubes**
- **1 box (10 ounces) frozen chopped spinach, thawed and squeezed dry**
- **¾ cup water**
- **1 tablespoon mango chutney**
- **⅓ cup yogurt, stirred with 1 teaspoon cornstarch**
- **For garnish: 1 medium-size Granny Smith apple, cored and chopped, and ⅓ cup peanuts**

1. Melt butter in a large skillet over medium heat. Add onion and cook 3 minutes, stirring occasionally, until nearly tender.

2. Stir in curry powder and lamb and cook 3 minutes, stirring occasionally, to blend flavors.

3. Stir in spinach, water and chutney. Bring to a simmer and cook 7 minutes, stirring occasionally, until mixture begins to thicken.

4. Stir in yogurt mixture and cook 3 minutes, stirring frequently, until hot.

5. Transfer to a heated platter. Garnish with apple and peanuts and serve.

Makes 4 servings. Per serving: 341 calories, 30 grams protein, 15 grams carbohydrate, 18 grams fat, 105 milligrams cholesterol with butter, 87 milligrams cholesterol with margarine, 180 milligrams sodium

Lamb with Spinach and Yogurt

Lamb Chops

Lamb chops may be cut from the loin, the rib (when left intact, this cut is the rack), the leg (often called lamb steaks) or the shoulder. Loin and rib chops are the most tender and expensive and are best simply grilled or broiled. Shoulder lamb chops are more economical and have excellent flavor. Two different chops are cut from the shoulder: arm chops, which have round bones, and shoulder blade chops, which have long bones. Either works well in the recipes that follow.

Lamb Chop—Potato Skillet

Add a green vegetable or a salad. For dessert, drizzle sliced ripe pears with a warm chocolate or hot-fudge sauce.

    4 tablespoons butter or margarine
    4 shoulder lamb chops, each about
        ¾-inch thick
    3 medium-size onions, sliced
    ½ teaspoon minced fresh garlic
About 1 cup chicken broth
    ¼ teaspoon dried rosemary leaves,
        crumbled
    ½ teaspoon salt
    4 medium-size all-purpose potatoes,
        scrubbed and sliced ¼-inch thick

1. Melt 2 tablespoons of the butter in a large skillet over medium-high heat until foamy. Add chops and brown on all sides. Transfer to a plate.

2. Add remaining 2 tablespoons butter to skillet and stir to scrape up browned bits on bottom of skillet. Add onions and garlic and cook 2 minutes, stirring frequently, until lightly browned.

3. Stir broth, rosemary and salt into skillet. Arrange a layer of potatoes over onion mixture. Place chops on top. Bring liquid to a boil. Reduce heat to low. Cover and simmer 35 minutes, adding more broth if needed to prevent scorching, until chops and potatoes are tender when pierced with a fork.

4. Serve from skillet or arrange on a heated platter and serve.

Makes 4 servings. Per serving: 709 calories, 31 grams protein, 29 grams carbohydrate, 52 grams fat, 159 milligrams cholesterol with butter, 123 milligrams cholesterol with margarine, 688 milligrams sodium

Dilled Lamb Chops, Carrots and Potatoes

This quick, colorful version of Irish stew is a whole meal cooked in one pot. If it's available in your market, substitute 1 tablespoon snipped fresh dill for the dillweed; stir it in at the end of the cooking time.

Four 7-ounce shoulder lamb chops
1¾ cups water
1½ teaspoons salt
    ¼ teaspoon pepper
1½ teaspoons dillweed
    8 small thin-skinned potatoes,
        scrubbed
    4 medium carrots, halved lengthwise
    1 package (1 ounce) white-sauce mix
    ½ cup milk

1. Arrange chops in a single layer in a Dutch oven. Add water, salt, pepper and ½ teaspoon of the dillweed. Bring to a boil over high heat. Reduce heat to low. Cover and simmer 10 minutes.

2. Add potatoes and carrots. Cover and simmer 20 minutes longer, until chops and vegetables are tender when pierced with a fork. Remove from heat.

3. Transfer chops and vegetables to a heated serving dish with a slotted spoon. Cover with a sheet of foil to keep warm.

4. Pour the cooking juices through a strainer and return 1½ cups juices to Dutch oven.

5. Whisk sauce mix and milk in a small bowl until well blended. Whisk into Dutch oven. Stir in remaining 1 teaspoon dillweed.

6. Place over medium heat and bring to a simmer, stirring or whisking constantly, until sauce is thickened and smooth.

7. Spoon sauce over chops and vegetables and serve.

Makes 4 servings. Per serving: 592 calories, 30 grams protein, 25 grams carbohydrate, 44 grams fat, 124 milligrams cholesterol, 940 milligrams sodium

Mixed Grill with Vegetables

3. Mix Italian dressing, mustard and rosemary in a small bowl with a fork. Brush half the mixture on meat and vegetables.

4. Broil meat and vegetables 3 to 4 inches from heat source 5 minutes. Turn everything and brush with remaining dressing mixture.

5. Broil 5 to 8 minutes longer, turning carrots and potatoes once more if needed to prevent burning, until sausages are well cooked and chops are done as desired.

6. Transfer meats and vegetables to a heated platter. Remove skins from onions, or let diners skin their own, and serve.

Makes 4 servings. Per serving: 597 calories, 34 grams protein, 26 grams carbohydrate, 39 grams fat, 131 milligrams cholesterol, 553 milligrams sodium

Lamb and Eggplant Dinner

Serve with rice and a tomato salad or stewed tomatoes.

Four 6-ounce shoulder lamb chops
 1 **small eggplant (about 1 pound), cut crosswise in ½-inch-thick slices**
 2 **large onions, cut in ½-inch-thick slices**
 ⅓ **cup bottled Italian dressing**
 2 **tablespoons butter or margarine**
Pepper to taste

1. Remove broiler pan from oven and grease rack. Turn on broiler.

2. Arrange chops, eggplant and onions on broiler-pan rack. Brush chops and eggplant with half the dressing. Dot onions with 1 tablespoon of the butter.

3. Broil 4 inches from heat source 5 minutes. Turn vegetables and chops. Brush chops and eggplant with remaining dressing; dot onions with remaining 1 tablespoon butter.

4. Broil 5 minutes longer, until chops are medium and eggplant and onions are tender and browned. Remove from heat. Season chops with pepper.

5. To serve: Arrange chops and overlapping slices of eggplant and onion on a heated platter or dinner plates.

Makes 4 servings. Per serving: 436 calories, 24 grams protein, 10 grams carbohydrate, 34 grams fat, 117 milligrams cholesterol with butter, 99 milligrams cholesterol with margarine, 536 milligrams sodium

Mixed Grill with Vegetables

The onion skins lift off easily once the onions are broiled.

Four 6-ounce shoulder lamb chops
 2 **sweet Italian sausages (about 3 ounces each), split lengthwise and cut in half crosswise**
 4 **small yellow onions, skins left on, cut in half crosswise**
 1 **can (16 ounces) whole white potatoes, drained**
 1 **box (10 ounces) frozen whole baby carrots, rinsed if needed to separate**
 ¼ **cup bottled Italian dressing**
 1 **tablespoon prepared mustard, preferably whole-grain**
 1 **teaspoon dried rosemary leaves**

1. Turn on broiler.

2. Arrange lamb chops, sausages and vegetables on broiler-pan rack, putting onions cut-side down.

Ribs and Shanks

🕙 **MAKE-AHEAD**
Grilled Lamb Ribs with Eggplant

Lamb ribs benefit from a little precooking to defat and tenderize, and a well-flavored marinade that clings to the meat. This marinade is also good on chicken breasts or beef or lamb kabobs.

5 pounds lamb-breast ribs or riblets,
    cut in 3-rib sections, trimmed of
    excess fat
Water
2 chicken bouillon cubes
½ teaspoon pepper
Two 2-inch-long bay leaves
½ cup olive oil
¼ cup lemon juice
¼ cup soy sauce or tamari
1 teaspoon dried basil leaves
¾ teaspoon dried oregano leaves
2 large cloves garlic
2 eggplants (about 1 pound each), cut
    in ½-inch-thick rounds

1. Put lamb ribs in a large pot or roasting pan with a lid. Add water just to cover meat. Add bouillon cubes, pepper and bay leaves. Cover and bring to a boil over high heat. Skim off foam that rises to the surface. Reduce heat to low. Cover and simmer 20 minutes. Remove from heat; let meat stand in cooking liquid 10 minutes.

2. Meanwhile, process oil, lemon juice, soy sauce, herbs and garlic in a food processor or a blender until smooth.

3. Drain ribs and pat dry with paper towels. Place in a large baking dish or double plastic food bag. Pour marinade over ribs. Turn ribs three or four times to coat well. Cover dish or close bag.

4. Refrigerate 1 to 2 hours, turning meat occasionally.

5. Prepare barbecue grill or turn on broiler.

6. Drain ribs; reserve marinade.

7. To grill: Place ribs directly on grill rack about 5 inches above medium-hot coals, meaty-side down. Cover barbecue grill with hood or cover ribs with a tent of heavy-duty foil and grill 10 minutes. (Grill 5 minutes longer if ribs are quite meaty.) Turn ribs and grill 5 minutes. Arrange eggplant on grill. Brush ribs and eggplant with some of the reserved marinade. Grill about 5 minutes. Turn eggplant; brush lamb and egg-plant with marinade. Grill 5 minutes longer, until lamb and eggplant are well browned and tender.

To broil: Arrange ribs meaty-side up on broiler-pan rack. Broil 6 inches from heat source 20 minutes, turning once. Arrange eggplant around ribs or in a shallow baking pan. Brush ribs and eggplant with some of the reserved marinade. Broil 5 minutes. Turn ribs and egg-plant; brush both with marinade and broil 5 minutes longer, until lamb and eggplant are well browned and tender. If broiler won't accommodate both pans at once, cook ribs first (a total of 30 minutes); cover and keep warm while egg-plant cooks (about 10 minutes).

8. Arrange ribs and eggplant on a heated plat-ter; provide plenty of napkins and serve.

Makes 4 servings. Per serving: 988 calories, 52 grams protein, 16 grams carbohydrate, 79 grams fat, 219 milligrams cholesterol, 989 milligrams sodium

---

Grilling with Herbs

Soak branches of fresh or dried aromatic herbs such as basil, thyme, tarragon, sage or oregano in cold water for about one hour. Drain well, then toss herbs onto hot coals just before adding foods to be grilled. Orange or lemon peels add delicate flavor to meat and vegetables, and the aroma is fantastic.

⏱ MAKE-AHEAD
Herb-Barbecued Lamb Ribs

Grill these ribs over low heat (see Grilling Tips, page 104).

4 pounds lamb-breast rib racks, trimmed of excess fat
½ cup white wine or water
¼ cup cider vinegar
1 small onion, minced
1 clove garlic, minced
1 teaspoon dried rosemary leaves, crumbled
1 teaspoon salt
½ teaspoon pepper
2 tablespoons olive or vegetable oil

1. Cut 1½-inch-deep slits between each rib or in meaty sides so marinade can penetrate. Mix wine, vinegar, onion, garlic, rosemary, salt and pepper in a roasting pan. Add ribs and brush with marinade. Cover and marinate overnight, turning ribs once or twice.

2. Prepare barbecue grill or heat oven to 350°F.

3. Drain ribs; reserve marinade. Brush ribs well on both sides with oil.

4. To grill: Arrange ribs on grill rack over low coals. Grill 45 minutes. Baste ribs with reserved marinade and grill about 30 minutes longer, basting and turning several times, until ribs are tender.

To roast: Place ribs on rack in a roasting pan. Roast 45 minutes. Baste ribs with reserved marinade and continue cooking as directed until tender.

5. Transfer ribs to a heated platter and serve.
Makes 4 servings. Per serving (with wine): 708 calories, 39 grams protein, 2 grams carbohydrate, 59 grams fat, 175 milligrams cholesterol, 687 milligrams sodium

California Barbecued Lamb Ribs

Grill these ribs over low heat (see Grilling Tips, page 104). Serve with a cucumber and red-onion salad and garlic bread.

4 pounds lamb-breast rib racks or riblets, trimmed of excess fat
1 teaspoon salt
½ teaspoon pepper
1 can (8 ounces) tomato sauce
2 tablespoons granulated sugar
2 tablespoons cider vinegar
1 teaspoon prepared mustard
1 teaspoon Worcestershire sauce
½ teaspoon crumbled dried thyme, tarragon or rosemary leaves
1 clove garlic, crushed
Dash of hot-pepper sauce

1. Prepare barbecue grill or heat oven to 350°F.

2. Cut 1½-inch-deep slits between each rib or in meaty sides so interior fat can drain off during cooking. Rub ribs with salt and pepper.

3. Mix tomato sauce, sugar, vinegar, mustard, Worcestershire sauce, thyme and garlic in a small bowl.

4. To grill: Arrange ribs directly on grill rack over low coals. Grill 45 minutes, turning occasionally. Baste with tomato-sauce mixture and grill 30 minutes longer, turning often and basting with sauce, until ribs are tender.

To roast: Arrange ribs on rack in a roasting pan. Bake 45 minutes; baste ribs and continue cooking as directed until ribs are tender.

5. Transfer ribs to a heated platter and serve.

Makes 4 servings. Per serving: 686 calories, 40 grams protein, 12 grams carbohydrate, 53 grams fat, 175 milligrams cholesterol, 1,060 milligrams sodium

Oven-Basted Lamb Shanks

Serve with crisp fried potatoes or hash browns and peas.

4 tablespoons all-purpose flour
8 large lamb shanks (about 1 pound each), trimmed of excess fat
1 tablespoon paprika
1 tablespoon dried parsley flakes
2 teaspoons instant minced onion
1 teaspoon onion powder
1 teaspoon garlic powder
1 teaspoon seasoned salt
1 teaspoon pepper
¾ cup dry sherry wine or beef broth
¾ cup water
For garnish: parsley sprigs and lemon wedges (optional)

1. Heat oven to 325°F. Have a large roasting pan ready.

2. Coat inside of each of two 16x10-inch roasting bags with ties with 1 tablespoon of the flour; shake out excess. Place bags in roasting pan. Place 4 lamb shanks fat-side up in each bag.

3. Mix remaining 2 tablespoons flour, the paprika, parsley, minced onion, onion and garlic powders, salt and pepper in a cup. Sprinkle evenly over lamb shanks. Stir together sherry and water; pour half into each bag. Rotate bags slightly to moisten seasonings.

4. Close bags and fasten tightly with ties. Cut 5 slits in top of each bag.

5. Roast 2 hours and 15 minutes, until lamb shanks are tender when pierced with a fork through a slit in the bag. Remove pan from oven. Cut bags open and let stand 5 minutes.

6. Transfer lamb shanks to a heated platter. Spoon gravy from bags over shanks. Garnish with parsley and lemon wedges, if desired, and serve.

Makes 8 servings. Per serving (with sherry): 568 calories, 51 grams protein, 3 grams carbohydrate, 38 grams fat, 195 milligrams cholesterol, 335 milligrams sodium

Wine-Braised Lamb Shanks

The initial oven-browning removes excess fat. Serve with canned cannelini beans, heated and seasoned with lemon juice, olive oil, chopped parsley, salt and pepper along with cherry tomatoes sauteed in butter.

4 lamb shanks (about 1 pound each)
1 teaspoon salt
½ teaspoon pepper
3 tablespoons all-purpose flour
1½ cups dry white wine
2 tablespoons chopped fresh parsley
2 tablespoons finely chopped onion
2 teaspoons minced fresh garlic
1 teaspoon grated fresh lemon peel
1 tablespoon freshly-squeezed lemon juice
½ teaspoon *each* dried thyme and rosemary leaves
For garnish: chopped fresh parsley

1. Heat oven to 350°F. Heavily grease a Dutch oven.

2. Season lamb shanks with salt and pepper. Coat with the flour and shake off excess. Arrange in a single layer in prepared Dutch oven.

3. Cover and bake about 2 hours, until lamb shanks are tender and browned. Remove from oven. Skim off and discard fat from pan juices.

4. Mix remaining ingredients except garnish in a small bowl. Pour over lamb shanks. Cover and bake about 35 minutes longer, until shanks are very tender. Remove from oven.

5. Transfer lamb shanks to a heated platter. Whisk pan juices to blend and pour over shanks. Sprinkle with parsley and serve.

Makes 4 servings. Per serving: 638 calories, 72 grams protein, 8 grams carbohydrate, 33 grams fat, 241 milligrams cholesterol, 731 milligrams sodium

Ground Lamb

Unlike ground beef, ground lamb is not labeled with the cut it is ground from or with the percentage of fat it contains. If meat looks white or light pink in color, it may contain a lot of fat; a deep red color indicates lean meat was used. Ground lamb is very perishable and should be cooked or wrapped tightly and frozen the day it's purchased. Ground beef can replace lamb in most recipes.

Greek Lamb Loaf

Look for bulgur wheat in supermarket health-food sections and Middle-Eastern food shops.

1½ pounds lean ground lamb
1 can (8 ounces) tomato sauce
1 cup fine-grind bulgur wheat
1 cup finely chopped onion
1 large egg
1 teaspoon ground allspice
¼ teaspoon pepper
⅓ cup Zante currants
4 tablespoons pignoli (pine nuts)

1. Heat oven to 350°F. Have ready a 12x7-inch or 9-inch-square baking pan.

2. Put lamb, tomato sauce, bulgur wheat, onion, allspice, pepper, currants and 2 tablespoons of the pignoli in a large bowl. Mix with a spoon until well blended.

3. Pat mixture evenly into baking pan. Score the top into diamonds. Sprinkle with remaining 2 tablespoons pignoli; press nuts lightly into the surface.

4. Bake 35 to 45 minutes, until meat loaf is lightly browned and a meat thermometer inserted in the center registers 160°F.

5. Remove from oven; let stand 5 minutes. Cut into squares and serve.

Makes 6 servings. Per serving: 439 calories, 24 grams protein, 30 grams carbohydrate, 25 grams fat, 120 milligrams cholesterol, 677 milligrams sodium

Lamb Patties with Vegetables Provençale

A whole meal made in a skillet. You may substitute ground beef for the lamb if you prefer.

1 pound lean ground lamb
1 large egg
2 tablespoons packaged dry bread crumbs
1¼ teaspoons salt
1 teaspoon crumbled dried rosemary leaves
Dash of hot-pepper sauce
1 tablespoon olive oil
1 medium-size onion, sliced in rings
2 large cloves garlic, crushed with the flat side of a heavy chef's knife
8 ounces zucchini, cut in ¼-inch slices
1 can (14½ ounces) tomatoes, undrained; tomatoes broken up
1 can (16 ounces) small whole potatoes, well drained
For garnish: minced fresh parsley

1. Mix lamb, egg, bread crumbs, 1 teaspoon of the salt, ¾ teaspoon of the rosemary and the hot-pepper sauce in a large bowl with hands or two forks. Shape mixture into 8 patties.

2. Heat oil in a large heavy skillet over high heat until hot but not smoking. Add lamb patties and cook about 2 minutes per side for medium. Remove from skillet with a slotted spoon to a plate.

3. Add onion and garlic to skillet. Reduce heat to medium and cook about 3 minutes, stirring occasionally, until onion is golden.

4. Stir zucchini and tomatoes into skillet. Season with remaining ¼ teaspoon salt and rosemary. Bring to a boil. Cover and simmer about 10 minutes, until zucchini is tender and flavors are blended.

5. Stir in potatoes. Arrange lamb patties on top of vegetables. Cover and cook just until potatoes are hot.

6. Remove from heat. Sprinkle with parsley and serve from skillet.

Makes 4 servings. Per serving: 468 calories, 23 grams protein, 21 grams carbohydrate, 32 grams fat, 144 milligrams cholesterol, 901 milligrams sodium

Meatball-and-Vegetable Skillet

- 2 tablespoons olive or vegetable oil
- 1 small eggplant (8 ounces), cut in ½-inch cubes (about 3 cups)
- 2 medium-size onions, thinly sliced (about 1½ cups)
- 1 teaspoon minced fresh garlic
- 2 medium-size zucchini (12 ounces), cut in ½-inch-thick rounds (about 2½ cups)
- 3 small carrots, thinly sliced (about ¾ cup)
- 6 ounces mushrooms, quartered (about 2¼ cups)
- 1 can (14½ ounces) stewed tomatoes
- 2 teaspoons fresh rosemary leaves or 1 teaspoon dried rosemary, crumbled
- ½ teaspoon salt
- ¼ teaspoon pepper
- 12 ounces lean ground lamb

1. Heat oil in a large deep skillet over medium-high heat. Add eggplant, onions and garlic. Cook 5 minutes, stirring two or three times, until onions are nearly tender and eggplant is lightly browned.

2. Add remaining ingredients except lamb to skillet. Bring to a boil. Reduce heat to low. Cover and simmer 5 minutes, until vegetables release their juices.

3. Meanwhile, form heaping tablespoons of lamb into 8 meatballs. Add meatballs to top of stew. Cover and cook 4 minutes.

4. Turn meatballs. Uncover and cook 4 to 6 minutes longer, until vegetables are tender and meatballs are no longer pink in the center when pierced with a knife. Remove from heat.

5. Spoon onto dinner plates and serve.

Makes 4 servings. Per serving: 334 calories, 20 grams protein, 18 grams carbohydrate, 21 grams fat, 60 milligrams cholesterol, 477 milligrams sodium

Microwave Method: Reduce amount of oil to 1 tablespoon and place in a 3-quart microwave-safe bowl. Add all ingredients except stewed tomatoes and lamb. Cover with a lid or vented plastic wrap. Microwave on high 12 to 14 minutes, stirring three times, until vegetables are crisp-tender. Meanwhile, shape lamb into meatballs as directed. Stir stewed tomatoes into vegetables; arrange meatballs around edge of bowl. Reduce power to medium-high. Cover and microwave 8 to 10 minutes, rotating dish ½ turn once, until meatballs are barely pink in center when pierced with the tip of a knife. Let stand 5 minutes, until meatballs are no longer pink and vegetables are tender.

Meatball-and-Vegetable Skillet

Savory Lamb with Cabbage

♥ LOW-CALORIE
Savory Lamb with Cabbage

Thaw frozen vegetables quickly by placing them in a strainer and rinsing under cold running water.

1¼	pounds lean ground lamb
1	can (11 ounces) condensed tomato and rice soup, undiluted
½	cup boiling water
1	box (10 ounces) frozen baby carrots, peas and pearl onions, thawed
½	teaspoon dried rosemary leaves
¼	teaspoon dried thyme leaves
¼	teaspoon salt
⅛	teaspoon pepper
1	pound green cabbage, shredded (about 6 cups)

1. Crumble lamb into a large skillet over high heat. Cook, stirring to break up large chunks, until lamb is no longer pink. Tilt skillet and spoon off excess fat.

2. Add soup, water, mixed vegetables, herbs, salt and pepper to lamb in skillet. Stir to mix well.

3. Top lamb mixture with cabbage. Cover and cook 10 minutes, until cabbage is crisp-tender.

4. Serve from skillet or spoon into a large heated bowl and serve.

Makes 4 servings. Per serving: 289 calories, 29 grams protein, 25 grams carbohydrate, 8 grams fat, 83 milligrams cholesterol, 858 milligrams sodium

Moussaka Stir-fry

Serve this quick version of a traditional Greek casserole over noodles.

1 **pound lean ground lamb**
1 **teaspoon garlic powder**
1 **teaspoon dried oregano leaves, crumbled**
¼ **teaspoon pepper**
½ **cup beef or chicken broth**
¼ **cup tomato paste**
¼ **cup sour cream**
3 **tablespoons olive oil**
8 **ounces Japanese or regular eggplant, cut crosswise in ¼-inch-thick slices (about 3 cups)**
1 **medium-size yellow, red or green bell pepper, cut in 1-inch chunks**
1 **cup frozen or fresh chopped onion**
1 **cup frozen green peas**
2 **ounces feta cheese, finely crumbled (½ cup)**

1. Mix lamb, garlic powder, oregano and pepper in a medium-size bowl with hands or a spoon until blended.

2. Mix broth, tomato paste and sour cream in a small bowl or a 2-cup measure until blended.

3. Place a Dutch oven over high heat 3 minutes, until very hot. Add 1 tablespoon of the oil. Tilt pot to coat bottom. Crumble in meat mixture and cook about 1 minute, stirring to break up chunks, until lamb is no longer pink. Spoon meat mixture and juices into a large bowl.

4. Heat remaining 2 tablespoons oil in Dutch oven. Add eggplant and stir-fry 2 to 3 minutes, until slightly softened. Add bell pepper and stir-fry 1 minute, until pepper is crisp-tender and eggplant is tender. Add to lamb mixture in bowl.

5. Add onion and green peas to Dutch oven. Stir-fry 1 minute, until thawed. Add broth mixture and bring to a boil. Boil 30 seconds, until mixture thickens.

6. Return lamb and vegetables to Dutch oven. Add feta cheese and stir 1 minute, until mixture is hot and evenly coated with sauce.

7. Spoon onto dinner plates and serve.

Makes 4 servings. Per serving: 443 calories, 40 grams protein, 17 grams carbohydrate, 24 grams fat, 134 milligrams cholesterol, 404 milligrams sodium

Moussaka Stir-fry

Ground-Lamb Patties with Tomatoes and Mozzarella

This delicious dinner is cooked in foil, cutting cleanup to a minimum. Bake all the packets at one time, or if everyone can't eat together, bake each packet as needed. A green salad with marinated artichoke hearts and whole-wheat rolls complete the menu.

1¼ **pounds lean ground lamb**
1 **teaspoon salt**
½ **teaspoon pepper**
2 **tablespoons vegetable oil**
½ **cup chicken broth**
¼ **cup chopped fresh parsley, mixed with 1 teaspoon minced fresh garlic**
4 **ounces mozzarella cheese, cut in 8 slices**
2 **small fresh tomatoes (about 4 ounces each), each cut in 6 slices**
1 **teaspoon chopped fresh rosemary leaves or ½ teaspoon dried rosemary**
1 **teaspoon chopped fresh oregano leaves or ½ teaspoon dried oregano**

1. Heat oven to 400°F. Have a baking sheet ready. Tear off four 12-inch squares of foil. Lightly spray one side of each with no-stick vegetable cooking spray or brush with a little vegetable oil.

2. Shape lamb into four 1-inch-thick oval-shape patties. Season with salt and pepper.

3. Heat oil in a large skillet over medium-high heat. Add lamb patties and cook 2 minutes per side, until browned. Place a patty on each square of foil.

4. Discard fat from skillet and add broth. Bring to a boil over high heat, stirring to scrape up browned bits on bottom of skillet. Boil 3 minutes, until broth is reduced to about ¼ cup. Remove from heat.

5. Sprinkle patties with parsley mixture. Top each with 2 slices cheese and 3 slices tomato, overlapping slices. Sprinkle with rosemary and oregano. Spoon reduced broth around each patty. Fold foil and seal edges securely. Arrange packets on baking sheet.

6. Bake 6 to 8 minutes, until lamb is medium. Open packets; transfer patties to plates and serve.

Makes 4 servings. Per serving: 260 calories, 31 grams protein, 6 grams carbohydrate, 12 grams fat, 106 milligrams cholesterol, 558 milligrams sodium

Ground-Lamb Ragout

Cinnamon and oregano add a Greek flair to this dish. Serve over rice or noodles or spoon into pita breads.

1 **tablespoon vegetable oil**
1 **large onion, chopped (about 1 cup)**
1 **pound lean ground lamb**
½ **teaspoon minced fresh garlic**
1 **can (15 ounces) tomato sauce**
1 **teaspoon dried oregano leaves**
¼ **teaspoon ground cinnamon**
1 **teaspoon salt**
¼ **teaspoon pepper**
¼ **cup chopped fresh parsley**
1 **cup plain low-fat yogurt, stirred smooth**

1. Heat oil in a large skillet over medium heat. Add onion and cook about 5 minutes, stirring occasionally, until tender.

2. Crumble lamb into skillet and add garlic. Increase heat to high and cook 3 to 5 minutes, stirring to break up chunks, until meat is no longer pink.

3. Stir tomato sauce, oregano, cinnamon, salt and pepper into skillet. Bring to a simmer. Reduce heat to medium. Simmer 15 minutes, stirring occasionally.

4. Remove from heat and stir in parsley and yogurt.

5. Heat mixture over low heat for 1 minute, stirring constantly, just until hot.

6. Serve from skillet or transfer to a heated bowl.

Makes 4 servings. Per serving: 233 calories, 20 grams protein, 15 grams carbohydrate, 10 grams fat, 63 milligrams cholesterol, 1,400 milligrams sodium

Veal

Always tender, with a delicate mild flavor that takes beautifully to rich flavorful sauces and fragrant herbs, veal is widely available today.

Veal in Casserole with Vegetables

Roasts and Chops

★ **SPECIAL—AND WORTH IT**

Stuffed Breast of Veal

A bone-in breast of veal weighs 9 to 10 pounds. Boned and stuffed, it serves 10 to 12, but you can buy a half or even less. The flank end of the breast is thin. For stuffing, look for the thicker brisket, which is more suitable for butterflying, and ask the butcher to bone it. You can stuff a breast of veal either by cutting between the meat and the ribs almost to the bottom to make a pocket or by removing all the bones and the white cartilage at the bottom and butterflying it (see illustrations on opposite page).

Frittata Stuffing

6 large eggs
3 tablespoons grated Romano cheese
1 tablespoon chopped fresh parsley
¼ teaspoon ground nutmeg
1 box (10 ounces) frozen chopped spinach, thawed and squeezed dry
1 tablespoon butter or margarine

Roast

2 cups vegetables from gravy, sautéed (see Best-Ever Gravy, page 10)
One 4½-pound veal breast, boned and butterflied (see illustration on opposite page), about 2½ pounds boned
6 slices (1 ounce each) Swiss cheese
6 slices (1 ounce each) mortadella or fully cooked ham (see Note)
½ teaspoon dried rosemary leaves, crumbled
⅛ teaspoon salt
⅛ teaspoon pepper
2 tablespoons butter or margarine
1½ cups dry white wine or water
Best-Ever Gravy (recipe, page 10)

1. To make stuffing: Beat eggs, cheese, parsley and nutmeg in a medium-size bowl until blended. Stir in spinach.

2. Melt butter in a large nonstick skillet over medium heat. Add egg mixture and cook about 4 minutes, until bottom and edges are set. Remove from heat. Frittata will continue to cook in the roast.

3. Heat oven to 350°F. Have ready a large roasting pan with the sautéed vegetables.

Stuffed Breast of Veal

4. To assemble roast: Open veal breast flat on work surface. Layer cheese and mortadella to within ½ inch of edges. Slide frittata out of skillet on top of cheese and mortadella. Trim edges to meet mortadella. Use frittata trimmings to fill in uncovered spots.

5. Roll up and tie with white string (see illustration, opposite page). Season top of roast with rosemary, salt and pepper. Place on sautéed vegetables in roasting pan. Dot top of roast with butter. Sprinkle with ½ cup of the wine.

6. Roast veal 1½ hours, sprinkling with remaining 1 cup wine and turning the meat three times, until a meat thermometer inserted in the thickest part, not touching stuffing, registers 170°F.

7. Remove roast to a heated platter. Cover with a loose foil tent to keep warm. Let stand 10 minutes. Meanwhile, make the gravy with pan juices.

8. Transfer roast to a cutting board and remove strings. Cut in thin slices and arrange on a heated platter. Serve with Best-Ever Gravy on the side.

Makes 12 servings meat, 1⅓ cups gravy. Per serving with 3 tablespoons gravy (with water and oil): 380 calories, 28 grams protein, 2 grams carbohydrate, 28 grams fat, 203 milligrams cholesterol with butter, 194 milligrams cholesterol with margarine, 477 milligrams sodium

Note: Mortadella is an Italian sausage originally made in Bologna. A fine-textured pork sausage studded with pieces of fat, it is found in the deli sections of gourmet-food shops and Italian-specialty stores.

Preparing a Stuffed Breast of Veal

Butterflying a Boned Breast of Veal: Hold meat flat on work surface with one hand while cutting through meat horizontally, working from thickest end to within ½ inch of opposite end. Open flat like a book or the wings of a butterfly.

Stuffing and Rolling: Arrange stuffing evenly over meat to within ½ inch of edges. Stuffing should be no more than 1-inch thick. Starting from one long side, roll up meat like a jelly roll. This makes a long, thin roast instead of a short, stubby one.

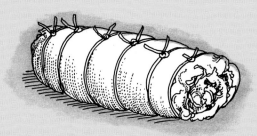

Tying: Measure length of rolled-up roast. Cut enough pieces of white string to tie roast about every ½ inch. Arrange strings lengthwise and evenly spaced on flat surface. Center roast on strings. Bring up and knot each string securely.

★ **SPECIAL—AND WORTH IT**
♥ **LOW-CALORIE**

Veal-Shoulder Roast

The largest muscle in the shoulder of veal is called the clod, but you won't see that term on a package at your supermarket. This solid piece of boneless meat weighs from 4 to 9 pounds, but you can buy a half. Have it tied for roasting or butterflied for a stuffed roast.

> 2 **cups vegetables from gravy, sautéed (see Best-Ever Gravy, page 10)**
> One 4-pound **boneless veal-shoulder roast, tied, trimmed of excess fat**
> 1 **teaspoon olive oil**
> 1 **teaspoon ground sage**
> ½ **teaspoon salt**
> ½ **teaspoon pepper**
> 1½ **cups water**
> ½ **cup dry white wine or additional water**
> **Best-Ever Gravy (recipe, page 10)**

1. Heat oven to 350°F. Have ready a medium-size roasting pan with the sautéed vegetables.

2. Rub roast with olive oil, sage, salt and pepper. Place on top of sautéed vegetables in roasting pan. Pour in ½ cup of the water. Mix remaining 1 cup water with wine and set aside.

3. Roast veal 2 to 2¼ hours, basting with wine mixture every 30 minutes and turning roast occasionally, until a meat thermometer inserted in the thickest part registers 170°F.

4. Transfer roast to a heated platter. Cover with a loose foil tent to keep warm. Let stand 10 minutes. Meanwhile, make the gravy with pan juices.

5. Transfer roast to a cutting board and remove strings. Carve in thin slices. Arrange on a heated platter. Serve with Best-Ever Gravy on the side.

Makes 8 servings meat with leftovers, 1½ cups gravy. Per 4-ounce serving with 3 tablespoons gravy (with water and oil): 266 calories, 31 grams protein, 1 gram carbohydrate, 14 grams fat, 119 milligrams cholesterol, 198 milligrams sodium

★ SPECIAL—AND WORTH IT

Veal in Casserole with Vegetables

(Shown on page 120)

In this one-pot company-special dish the vegetables cook with the meat. Start the meal with a creamy spinach or broccoli soup and finish with your favorite chocolate cake. Slice leftover meat thin and serve cold.

2 tablespoons butter or margarine
One 3-pound boneless rolled veal-
     shoulder or rump roast, tied,
     trimmed of excess fat
1 teaspoon salt
¼ teaspoon pepper
¼ teaspoon *each* dried thyme and
     rosemary leaves
1 cup chicken broth
1 cup tomato juice
1 cup *each* finely chopped onion
     and celery
1 small bay leaf
6 medium-size carrots, cut in chunks
6 small thin-skinned potatoes,
     scrubbed (about 12 ounces)
8 ounces mushrooms, sliced (about
     2 cups)
3 medium-size parsnips, cut in chunks
1 can (14½ ounces) tomatoes, well
     drained
For garnish: parsley sprigs

1. Heat butter in a large range-top casserole or Dutch oven over medium heat until foamy. Add veal and cook 10 to 15 minutes, turning often to brown all sides. Remove from heat and drain off butter.

2. Meanwhile, heat oven to 325°F.

3. Season veal with salt, pepper, thyme and rosemary. Add chicken broth, tomato juice, onion, celery and bay leaf to casserole. Bring to a boil over medium heat.

4. Cover casserole and transfer to oven. Bake 45 minutes.

5. Add carrots, potatoes, mushrooms and parsnips to casserole. Cover and bake 30 minutes.

6. Add tomatoes. Cover and bake 15 minutes longer, until veal and vegetables are tender. Remove from oven.

7. Transfer veal to a cutting board. Let stand 10 minutes. Remove vegetables to a heated platter with a slotted spoon. Cover loosely with a foil tent to keep warm.

8. Discard bay leaf. Bring pan juices to a boil over high heat and boil about 5 minutes, stirring to scrape up browned bits on bottom of casserole, until reduced by half.

9. Remove strings from veal. Cut in thin slices and arrange on platter with vegetables. Spoon some sauce over meat and garnish with parsley sprigs. Pour remaining sauce into a sauceboat to pass on the side.

Makes 6 servings with leftover meat. Per 3½-ounce serving meat with vegetables and sauce: 358 calories, 33 grams protein, 27 grams carbohydrate, 14 grams fat, 103 milligrams cholesterol with butter, 99 milligrams cholesterol with margarine, 823 milligrams sodium

Veal Paprikash

This can also be made with leftover pork roast. Serve over broad egg noodles.

2 tablespoons butter or margarine
1½ cups chopped onions
1 large green bell pepper, chopped (about 1 cup)
2 tablespoons paprika
1 can (14½ to 16 ounces) tomatoes,
     drained and chopped
12 ounces cooked veal-shoulder or
     other veal roast, sliced ¼-inch
     thick, then cut in thin strips
½ cup water
½ teaspoon salt
½ teaspoon pepper
¾ cup sour cream (see Cooking with Yogurt and
     Sour Cream, page 70)

1. Melt butter in a large skillet over medium heat. Add onions and bell pepper and cook about 4 minutes, stirring frequently, until crisp-tender. Stir in paprika and cook 2 minutes to develop flavor.

2. Add tomatoes, veal, water, salt and pepper. Bring to a simmer and cook about 7 minutes, stirring occasionally, until thickened. Stir in sour cream and remove from heat.

3. Transfer to a heated platter and serve.

Makes 4 servings. Per serving: 381 calories, 27 grams protein, 14 grams carbohydrate, 25 grams fat, 123 milligrams cholesterol with butter, 105 milligrams cholesterol with margarine, 560 milligrams sodium

🕐 **MAKE-AHEAD**

★ **SPECIAL—AND WORTH IT**

Grilled Veal Chops with Sauce Italienne

Serve with lightly buttered spinach pasta and baby carrots. Veal chops are a bit pricy, so save this recipe for a special occasion. You can also make this dish with pork chops, if you prefer, but be sure to cook them to an internal temperature of 160°F.

Four 12-ounce loin veal chops, 1- to
  1¼-inches thick, trimmed of
  excess fat
½ teaspoon garlic powder
½ teaspoon salt
¼ teaspoon pepper
1½ tablespoons fresh-squeezed lemon
  juice
Sauce Italienne (recipe follows)

1. Arrange veal chops in a single layer in a shallow baking dish. Season both sides with the garlic powder, salt and pepper. Drizzle with lemon juice. Cover dish and marinate chops in refrigerator up to 6 hours.

2. Remove from refrigerator and let stand at room temperature for 30 minutes.

3. Prepare barbecue grill or turn on broiler.

4. To grill: Arrange chops directly on grill rack 4 to 6 inches above hot coals. Grill 7 to 9 minutes per side, until a meat thermometer inserted in the thickest part registers 140°F for medium-rare.

To broil: Arrange chops on broiler-pan rack. Broil 4 to 5 inches from heat source 7 to 9 minutes per side, until chops test done as described.

5. Transfer chops to dinner plates or a heated platter. Top each with ¼ cup Sauce Italienne and serve.

Makes 4 servings. Per serving with ¼ cup sauce: 515 calories, 54 grams protein, 5 grams carbohydrate, 29 grams fat, 209 milligrams cholesterol with butter, 204 milligrams cholesterol with margarine, 628 milligrams sodium

Sauce Italienne

2 tablespoons butter or margarine
1 tablespoon olive oil
1½ cups finely chopped green onions
1 teaspoon minced fresh garlic
2 cans (16 ounces each) tomatoes in
  purée, undrained; tomatoes
  broken up
1 teaspoon chopped fresh basil leaves
  or ½ teaspoon dried basil
½ teaspoon salt
½ teaspoon granulated sugar
½ teaspoon pepper

1. Heat butter and oil in a large heavy saucepan (not uncoated aluminum) over medium-high heat. Stir in onions and garlic and cook 5 minutes, stirring occasionally, until onions are tender.

2. Stir in tomatoes, basil, salt, sugar and pepper and bring to a boil, stirring occasionally. Reduce heat to low.

3. Simmer sauce 30 minutes, stirring occasionally, until sauce is slightly thickened and flavors have blended. Remove from heat.

4. Taste sauce and correct seasonings if necessary. Serve hot.

Makes 4 cups. Per ¼ cup: 42 calories, 1 gram protein, 5 grams carbohydrate, 2 grams fat, 5 milligrams cholesterol with butter, 0 milligrams cholesterol with margarine, 231 milligrams sodium

Note: This recipe makes a big batch of sauce, handy to have available to use in other recipes or over pasta. Refrigerate leftover sauce up to 4 days or freeze in meal-size portions up to 6 months.

Liver

Calves' Liver with Braised Leeks and Mushrooms

Cremini mushrooms are light tan to dark brown and have a deep, earthy flavor. But regular white button mushrooms work fine in this recipe, too.

Four 4-ounce slices calves' liver,
    ½-inch thick
¾ teaspoon salt
⅓ cup all-purpose flour
3 tablespoons olive oil
3 small leeks, white part only, cut in
    thin 2-inch-long strips, then
    rinsed well to remove grit (about
    2½ cups)
8 ounces mushrooms, preferably
    Cremini, sliced (about 4 cups)
¼ cup dry white wine (optional)

1. Season liver with ¼ teaspoon of the salt. Put flour on a sheet of waxed paper and coat liver in flour.

2. Heat 2 tablespoons of the oil in a large skillet over medium-high heat until hot but not smoking. Add liver to skillet and fry 2 minutes per side, until golden brown outside but pink in the center. Remove to a heated platter and cover loosely with a sheet of foil to keep warm.

3. Heat remaining 1 tablespoon oil in skillet. Add leeks and cook about 1 minute, stirring constantly, until barely wilted.

4. Stir in mushrooms and remaining ½ teaspoon salt. Stir-fry 4 to 5 minutes, until mushrooms are tender.

5. Add wine to skillet, if desired, and bring to a boil. Remove from heat. Spoon mushroom mixture over liver and serve.

Makes 4 servings. Per serving (without wine): 340 calories, 25 grams protein, 24 grams carbohydrate, 16 grams fat, 341 milligrams cholesterol, 51 milligrams sodium

Liver and Peppers Venetian Style

You can use beef liver instead of calves' liver if you prefer.

1 large onion, halved lengthwise and
    thinly sliced
6 slices bacon, cut crosswise in thin
    strips
1½ pounds trimmed sliced calves' liver,
    cut crosswise in ¼-inch-wide
    strips
2 tablespoons all-purpose flour
¼ cup water
3 tablespoons red-wine vinegar
1½ teaspoons dried oregano leaves
⅛ teaspoon pepper
1 jar (7 ounces) roasted red peppers,
    drained and cut in thin strips

1. Cook onion and bacon in a large skillet over medium heat 6 minutes, stirring occasionally, until onion is lightly browned and bacon is crisp.

2. Remove onion mixture to a bowl with a slotted spoon. Pour off all but 2 tablespoons fat from skillet.

3. Sprinkle liver strips with flour and toss to coat. Add liver to skillet and cook 8 minutes, stirring often with a fork to separate pieces, until browned.

4. Add water, vinegar, oregano and pepper to skillet and stir to blend. Add onion-bacon mixture and roasted peppers. Cook 4 minutes, stirring occasionally, until mixture is hot and sauce has thickened.

5. Transfer to a heated platter and serve.

Makes 6 servings. Per serving: 259 calories, 26 grams protein, 13 grams carbohydrate, 11 grams fat, 503 milligrams cholesterol, 215 milligrams sodium

Index